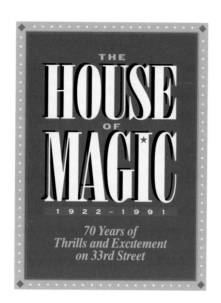

THE
HOUSE
OF
MAGIC
1922-1991

*70 Years of
Thrills and Excitement
on 33rd Street*

Acknowledgements

Editor: Bob Brown, Orioles
Printed in USA by French Bray, Inc.
Designed by Beshara Associates, Inc.
Library of Congress Cataloging in Publication Data
©1991 The Orioles, Inc. All rights reserved.
ISBN #0-9629565-0-3
House of Magic

Special Recognition

John Steadman, Gordon Beard, Jim Bready, Harry Dalton, Bruce Genther,
Jim Henneman, Frank Lynch, Bob Maisel, Bot Roda, Morton Tadder (Last
Opening Day), Sam Carnahan (Last Opening Day), Janis Rettaliata (Lost
Weekend), Joe Giza (Front Cover), Jerry Wachter

Richard S. Armstong, Babe Ruth Museum, Helen Conklin, Peter Curtis, Jeffrey Oh,
Ted Patterson, Don Schnably, Richard Waldrep, Phil Wood, John Ziemann

Contributing Photographers

J. Pat Carter, Amy Davis - Baltimore Sun (page 109), Joe DiPaola,
Joe Giza, Tom Gregory (Title Page), Hearst Corporation, Paul Hutchins -
Baltimore Sun (page 20), Mitchell Layton, Hugh McNally, LeRoy Merriken,
Janis Rettaliata, Jay Spencer, Tom Sullivan, Gene Sweeney, Jr -
Baltimore Sun (page 105), Morton Tadder, Jerry Wachter, John Weiss

Table of Contents

THE First Opening Day

BY JIM BREADY

Which was the greatest baseball game ever played at Memorial Stadium? There have been some keen arguments over that one, as the 1991 season ends and, with it, the Orioles' stadium tenancy. Some fans will no doubt nominate the 1958 game when Hoyt Wilhelm no-hit, no-runned the champion Yankees. Others, the 1966 game when Frank Robinson smote the one home run in stadium history that carried clear over the wall and out into the parking lot. Or, that same year, Game Four in the Orioles' first, victorious World Series, the upset sweep Series. Gr-r-r-reat games, those; and many another besides, among 3,000-plus home games altogether.

But this is to stake a claim for the one on Thursday, April 15, 1954; the very first baseball game played at Memorial Stadium.

It was Baltimore 3, Chicago 1 that overcast afternoon; the proceedings included a vast opening-day turnout and two home runs, but nothing for baseball's all-time record books.

Why was it so special? Because the last previous major league baseball game played in Baltimore was on September 29, 1902.

Today's fan calls the five months between seasons a long wait. A few of the people in the seats that day in Easter Week marveled at having lived long enough to be there, to watch and enjoy such an event. They had been waiting 51 1/2 years.

The club-owner vote to readmit Baltimore to the American League (which Baltimore had helped found, in 1901) occurred the previous September, in New York. Throughout that 1902-to-1953 interim, all eight A.L. franchises had been bolted to

bedrock. The National League, similarly motionless, finally in 1953 allowed the Braves to quit Boston for Milwaukee. Nevertheless, for the American League, the idea of taking a failed team out of St. Louis, of relocating it in this more hospitable setting, was revolutionary.

Since then, transfer and expansion have brought big league baseball to a full dozen new cities, in this country and Canada; two more new N.L. franchises are on the way. But in 1954, when, at last, shrewd maneuvers worked and wildest dreams came true, Baltimore, without quite knowing it, turned into a wholly different city. The first, official, major league pitch (by Bullet Bob Turley) was enough to invest the day with historical meaning. Then when the last pitch (Turley was still going strong) added the grace note of scoreboard victory by the Orioles, those of us who were there reached a high like none other since.

Two men took the lead in having a new ballpark ready, in rounding up the purchase money, and in convincing the American League owners. One was Thomas D'Alesandro Jr., the mayor from Little Italy; the other, Clarence W. Miles, a Shoreman, corporation lawyer and Guilford socialite. None of it came easily. Three bond-loan votes were necessary to foot the $6,500,000 bill for on-again, off-again construction at this two-deck, roofless, open-end, real-grass stadium that would be Baltimore's memorial to the combat dead of World War II; this baseball-configuration stadium was built with no assurance that the A.L. or N.L. would ever use it. Behind the scenes, the moguls of local commerce and industry had to be prodded into putting up the $2,475,000 required for buyout (how small a sum it looks today). The Washington Senators were quietly paid off for this territorial-rights incursion; money and a front-office job went to Jack Dunn III, the owner of Baltimore's existing minor league franchise.

As the reborn Orioles opened spring training at Yuma, Arizona, as Deluca-Davis and Joseph F.

VICE-PRESIDENT RICHARD M. NIXON, SUBBING FOR PRESIDENT DWIGHT D. EISENHOWER, THROWS OUT THE FIRST BALL AT THE FIRST HOME OPENER. HE IS FLANKED HERE BY ORIOLES CLUB PRESIDENT CLARENCE MILES, (LEFT) AND MARYLAND GOVERNOR THEODORE MCKELDIN.

★

Hughes Co. fought the weather to finish work on the stadium in time, as floats were built for a splendiferous parade the morning of the home opener, the nation watched, with interest. The schedule had the new team playing its first two games in Detroit; for the opener at Briggs Stadium, attendance unexpectedly topped that at every other park in the majors. Then the Orioles, 1-1 in the standings, headed for home. The New Yorker and Life magazines, the wire services, the broadcast networks allotted gratifying lines and minutes. Baltimore's most widely read columnist, Lou Azrael of the News-Post, had gone to Italy on vacation; at a Venice hotel, he ran into Ernest Hemingway. They had known each other as fellow-correspondents in WWII. Hemingway hoped

PLAYERS LINE UP FOR THE NATIONAL ANTHEM, SUNG BY ELWOOD GARY, AS JIM BREADY SAYS, INTO A DEAD MIKE.

★

the Orioles would do well—still, he asked, why had they offered no contract to the old but famous Browns pitcher, Satchel Paige?

On the great day, many businesses closed; City Hall ordained a half-holiday; "No School!" said the School Board. It was 58 degrees, and drizzling; regardless, 76 minutes' and 22 marching bands' worth of parade, before some 350,000 spectators, stepped off promptly at 10:30 a.m. Army jeeps from Fort Meade towed the floats. The route lay from 34th Street down Charles to Madison, over to Howard, and east on Baltimore—56 blocks. Gov. Theodore R. McKeldin and many another politico were in the line; Ford Frick, Organized Baseball's commissioner; Connie Mack and Clark Griffith, representing Philadelphia and Washington; Bill Clarke, Jack Doyle, Charlie

Harris and Mrs. John McGraw, representing the 1890s National League Orioles. The parade's highlight, though, was the new-age Baltimore Orioles.

The 25 players, traveling in 1954 by train, arrived at 9:45 a.m., at the B&O's Camden Station. They had suited up while still aboard; then, in top-down convertibles, three to a car, they were driven north to the parade's marshaling area in uniform, but wearing their street shoes. Here was drama—a city having its very first look at this, its very own modern-majors team. The signal came: Go! And behold—the Orioles, big as life, glided along, smilingly tossing 10,000 plastic baseballs to the frantic, pleading hands. Passing Sun Square, the players were enveloped in shredded paper; the office canyons reverberated. Passing City Hall, the parade's terminus, the convertibles speeded up, and made for the ballpark. Game time was approaching.

It was, correspondingly, the players' first look at

THE TWO MANAGERS, CHICAGO'S PAUL RICHARDS AND THE ORIOLES' JIMMY DYKES ENGAGE IN A PRE-GAME HANDSHAKE.

★

G.M. ART EHLERS AND MANAGER DYKES HEAD FOR THE BALLPARK IN THEIR BUICK CONVERT- IBLE AFTER PARADE ENDED AT CITY HALL.

★

their new home. "We stood there and stared," Gil Coan recalled, 37 years later (on the great day, he was the Orioles' starting centerfielder). "That huge concrete oval didn't look much like a ballpark. That outfield—to play it right, you'd need *five* outfielders.

"We had long-ball hitters—Mele, Wertz, Courtney. But what they hit, fair or foul, were going to be long, high outs." At that moment, a tarpaulin covered the infield, meaning no batting practice, just battery warmups. As Elwood Gary sang the Star-Spangled Banner (into a dead microphone), the two teams were aligned, heads bared, along first-and-third-base lines.

A few hundred bleacher seats had gone on sale that morning (bleachers, 75 cents—50 cents if under age 12; box seats, $3; lot parking, 25 cents; 36-page program with printed batting order, 15 cents). In the broadcasting booth were Ernie Harwell and Bailey Goss; nearby, general manager Art Ehlers. In the stands, Mayor D'Alesandro

★

1954 OPENING DAY PROGRAM/SCORECARD.

was absent, owing to a protracted hospitalization (one visitor, at Bon Secours, had been Clarence W. Miles, who as club president presented Tommy with a lifetime pass to all Orioles home games). Also missing was President Eisenhower, who had promised himself a Georgia golfing vacation; his replacement, the man who had gone beforehand from car to parade car shaking players hands, was Vice President Nixon. Thus, at the stadium, a Navy veteran rather than a former soldier, took the military dedication salutes; and when it came time for the first-ball ceremony, from a front-row seat, it was Richard M. Nixon who reared back and threw.

The man who then cried "Play ball!" was Baltimore's Eddie Rommel. In youth, to go big league, he had left town, joining Philadephia's A's. Once in his 13 years as a tall, strong righthander, Edwin Americus Rommel had won 27 games; once he won a World Series game. Now he was an A.L. umpire.

First up was Chico Carrasquel, at shortstop for the White Sox; he singled, but was left on base. The home team's first batter was another Baltimorean—Bobby Young, second baseman earlier for the International League Orioles; he flied out. But, that same inning, Coan walked, to

THE FIRST PITCH IN MEMORIAL STADIUM HISTORY, TO WHITE SOX LEAD OFF MAN CHICO CARRASQUEL.

★

TWO OF THE GAME'S GREATEST PATRIARCHS RIDE IN THE PRE-GAME PARADE, 84-YEAR OLD CLARK GRIFFITH, THE WASHINGTON SENATORS OWNER, AND PHILADEL- PHIA A'S FOUNDER AND OWNER 91-YEAR OLD CONNIE MACK.

★

become the first of all modern-Orioles baserunners in Baltimore. No names on the shirtbacks, then, just numerals; the fans set out to memorize the numbers for Jimmy Dykes, aged 57, the manager; 23-year-old Turley (no radar gun at 1950s games, but he threw consistently in the 90s); Don Larsen, not yet famous, who had pitched well in Detroit; Chuck Diering, the outfielder voted at season end the team's most valuable player; the bespectacled catcher, Clint Courtney (known as Scrap Iron for his willingness to fight with anybody over anything).

In the third, it was Courtney who scored the game's—and the team's—first run, homering to right. In the fourth inning, third baseman Vern Stephens hit one into the left field bleachers. There would be only 17 more Orioles homers at cavernous Memorial Stadium that year, and only 15 in all of the following season. The insurance run came on a single by Wertz. Turley, meanwhile, was fanning nine batters, allowing seven hits and yielding a lone run. Three of the home team's nine hits were by first baseman Eddie Waitkus. The White Sox (featuring Bob Boyd and Minnie Minoso, and managed by Paul Richards, who used three pitchers that day) threatened, but never caught

CLINT COURTNEY, VERN STEPHENS AND WINNING
PITCHER BOB TURLEY WHO WENT THE ROUTE TO
BEAT THE WHITE SOX, 3-1.

up. Which, as the clock passed 5 p.m., was just as well: The game couldn't go into extra innings, not with the lighting towers still unfinished.

Ironic, that the label for city classification—major league, minor league—should have originated with baseball. The first big league formed in 1871; Baltimore was there in the standings, sometimes atop them, across the next three decades. Then, for half a century, Baltimore alone among the five principal cities of the Northeast bore the stigma, the unfairness of minor-league existence. A city thus degraded suffers psychologically—while its old rivals undertake big construction projects and pile up civic achievements, the minor league city retreats into insularity and defensiveness, underlain with an inferiority complex. Such a city thinks, finances, builds, dares small. On its newspaper sports pages, from day to day, the accounts of faraway big league baseball games rate larger headlines than do the successes of its own International League team.

Once a city does attain the status—with a framed certificate as proof—of big league membership, there is no guarantee of permanence, any more than there was in 1901 and 1902. Baltimore for one has the handicap of a small hinterland. And U.S. population drift toward the south and west, plus immigration, has resulted in a belt of swelling cities with franchise ambitions. A 1991 fan, skimming over the coverage of that glorious day in 1954, finds other sports franchises represented in the parade, and flinches: Baltimore Colts, Baltimore Bullets, Baltimore Rockets. Just names, nowadays.

There was strong competition for the American League's unstuck franchise, back there in 1953 and 1954. But Baltimore, with Maryland behind it, won. And ever since, the actuality of being once again where we belong, in the Majors, has infused our planners, our doers—many of whom leave other metropolitan centers to work and live here. In its skyline, its after-work preoccupations and especially its self-respect, Baltimore stands transformed. You are free, contemplating that upsurge, to choose your own symbol for it.

For me, it's an afternoon of baseball, 37 years ago.

ONE OF MANY HISTORIC MOMENTS ON THAT DAY, APRIL 15, 1954. ORIOLES CATCHER CLINT COURTNEY ABOUT TO CROSS HOME PLATE AFTER HITTING THE FIRST HOME RUN IN MEMORIAL STADIUM HISTORY. THE VICTIM WAS THE WHITE SOX STARTER VIRGIL TRUCKS.

★

THE

Paul Richards

YEARS

BY BOB MAISEL

The assignment was, "Write a story about the Paul Richards era in Orioles baseball." Put another way, it could have been, "Tell how the Orioles went from the bedraggled St. Louis Browns they inherited in 1954 to an organization that was to become a force in the American League for most of the next 30 years." In 1953, their last year in St Louis, the Browns finished 54-100 and were 46 1/2 games behind the pennant winning New York Yankees. On Oct. 29 of that year, the franchise was transferred to Baltimore, and in their first season the Orioles again went 54-100, this time 57 games behind the first place Cleveland Indians. Beneath that uniform shirt that said Orioles, they were still, in effect, the St Louis Browns.

There was one significant change made,

however, one that would have a lot to say about the Orioles' future. On Sep. 14 of that first season, Paul Richards, manager of the opposition on the day of that historic first game at Memorial Stadium, left the White Sox and signed on as manager-general manager of the Orioles, replacing Jimmy Dykes and Arthur Ehlers. Dykes managed out the rest of the season, Ehlers accepted another job in the organization and was a valuable member of it until his death.

But, Richards, with as fine a baseball mind as I've had the privilege of observing first-hand in a lifetime of being around the game, proved to be exactly what a building franchise in a new town needed to become competitive with as little lost motion as possible. Many additional excellent baseball people such as longtime farm director Jim McLaughlin, Lee

TRAVELING SECRETARY JACK DUNN III AND RICHARDS STAGE A PHOTO THE DAY PAUL SIGNED WITH THE ORIOLES AS MANAGER-GENERAL MANAGER IN SEP '54...THE DUNN FAMILY NAME HAS BEEN SYNONYMOUS WITH PROFESSIONAL BASEBALL IN BALTIMORE SINCE JACK'S GRANDFATHER BOUGHT THE INTERNATIONAL LEAGUE ORIOLES BACK IN THE EARLY 1900S, AND LATER MANAGED THEM TO A RECORD SEVEN STRAIGHT PENNANTS ('19-'25)...JACK III LATER SERVED AS RICHARDS' RIGHT HAND MAN IN HIS CAPACITY OF ASSISTANT GENERAL MANAGER.

★

MacPhail, Harry Dalton, Frank Cashen, Earl Weaver, Hank Bauer, Hank Peters, Roland Hemond, Frank Robinson, Cal Ripken, Sr., among others, put their stamp on the finished product through the years, but it was Paul Richards' regime which laid the groundwork, and provided the system which others followed.

My first question to Richards when he came to Baltimore was, "How do you go about reviving a franchise that has just lost 100 games two seasons in a row?" His answer was, "The first thing you do is improve the pitching and defense. They keep you in games, give you a chance to win. The closer you can keep the score, the better chance there is that you can do something to win, which also keeps the fans more interested, gives them some reason for hope.

"While you're doing that, you improve your scouting and your farm system, sign as many prospects as you can and get them up to the big leagues as soon as possible. That way, you gradually add players who have offensive ability as well as defensive, and the combination makes you competitive. Usually, the toughest thing to come up with, the ingredient that puts you over the hump, is to mix in what I call a couple of animals, players who do it all...offense, defense and hit with power. Put all that together and you've got a champion." It was the exact formula he followed, and although he never won a pennant before moving on near the end of the 1961 season, he made the organization competitive, set the tone both on the field and in the front office, and the Orioles were on their way.

The next few seasons were a blur of activity. Fifty-four different players wore the Orioles uniform in 1955 alone. One of the first things

Richards did in the off-season after taking charge in '54, was execute the biggest trade in Orioles (if not baseball) history. There were 17 names involved. Paul sent Bob Turley, Don Larsen, Billy Hunter, Mike Blyzka, Darrell Johnson, Dick Kryhoski, Ted del Guercio, and Jim Fridley to the Yankees for catchers Gus Triandos and Hal Smith, shortstop Willie Miranda, outfielder Gene Woodling, pitchers Harry Byrd, Jim McDonald, and Bill Miller, infielders Don Leppert and Kal Segrist.

If one of his stated first objectives was to improve pitching, it didn't seem logical that trading away arms such as Turley and Larsen was the way to go about it. Richards's explanation was, "Right now we need numbers and we need catching. There isn't much in the farm system. Anyway, I think I can do a few things to help the pitching until we develop some of our own."

If Richards was a well-rounded baseball man, his strong point probably was working with pitchers,

★
SHORTSTOP WILLY MIRANDA JOINED THE ORIOLES IN THE "17 PLAYER DEAL" FROM THE YANKEES, AND BECAME ONE OF THE CLUB'S FIRST FAN FAVORITES...THE PERSONABLE CUBAN FAMED FOR HIS FANCY GLOVEWORK RECIPROCATED THEIR AFFECTION. HE STILL LIVES IN BALTIMORE MORE THAN 35 YEARS LATER.

getting another year or two out of veterans and force-feeding the young ones with live arms. He improved the pitching the first few years by bringing in veterans, giving them another pitch (his favorite an offspeed delivery with a sinking action he called the "slip" pitch), and rebuilding their confidence.

Bill Wight and George Zuverink added sinkers and were effective; Harry Dorish polished his changeup and helped; Jim Wilson came from the White Sox and won 12 games; Ray Moore from the

PAUL DEMONSTRATES "SLIP PITCH" GRIP TO A COUPLE OF VETERAN HURLERS GEORGE ZUVERINK AND JACK HARSHMAN.

★

Dodgers system to win 10, and so on. But, with no help from the farm system, 1955 was still a struggle. Richards said later he managed harder that year than any other time in his career, because he didn't want the club to lose 100 games again. It didn't quite, winding up 57-97, 39 games out of first.

You could start to see improvement in 1956. The infield was decent defensively with Bob Boyd at first, Billy Gardner second, Miranda short, George Kell at third, and Triandos and Smith handling the catching. And, Skinny Brown, Connie Johnson, Don Ferrarese, and Mike Fornieles added to the pitching depth. Tito Francona developed with the bat and defensively in the outfield; Dick Williams and Bob Nieman produced some offense. The record improved to 69-85. Richards was borrowing time while the farm system matured.

As with everything else he did, Richards had

a definite plan for developing the farm system. He was the first I saw who brought all of the minor league managers to training camp. The reasoning was that not only could they get better acquainted with the players they would manage some day, but they could also be taught how he wanted the game played.

He and pitching coach Harry Brecheen worked with the young pitchers, while at the same time letting the farm club managers know exactly what was wanted in the way of instruction to pitchers throughout the system. By the time farm managers left for their own camps, they knew the way rundowns and pick-off plays were to be handled, where cutoff men should be positioned, how to run the bases, etc.

In other words, fundamentals were to be taught the same at every level, so that when a player went from one team to another on his way up, nothing was new to him. He was always on familiar ground. Sounds simple, except that some organizations still don't operate that way today. Young players have to relearn fundamentals at every stop, and it wastes time.

AMONG THE PROSPECTS SIGNED EARLY IN THE RICHARDS ADMINISTRATION WAS THIS YOUNGSTER FROM LITTLE ROCK, AR.

Just a few years before he died, when Richards was scouting and working with the Texas Rangers, I sat with him at an exhibition game. Elrod Hendricks walked over and said, "Good to see you Mr. Richards. I just want to tell you that the system you put in here a long time ago is the same one we use today. It's still the greatest."

When Hendricks left, Richards said, "It was nice of him to say that. It's good to hear. Funny thing is I can't get it into our own organization."

As mentioned before, Richards knew the farm system had been barren when he arrived and needed both numbers and quality. He signed many young players, including bonus players, while continuing to make trades. He made mistakes along the way, and spent more money than some of the owners and members of the board thought prudent. His critics complained about the "buckshot" approach he used to sign players, but you can't argue with the results. The farm system started to produce, and it was gradually reflected in the standings.

In 1957 a milestone was achieved. For the first time the Orioles won as many as they lost, finishing at 76-76, but still 21 games out of first. Some interesting things happened on the field that year,

★
BILLY O'DELL, THE '58 ALL-
STAR GAME MVP, CON-
GRATULATED BY THE
YANKEES GIL MCDOUGALD
AND WHITE SOX'
NELLIE FOX.

including one of the weirdest finishes to any Orioles game ever.

On May 18 the White Sox were leading 4-3 just seconds before a 10:20 p.m. curfew, which had been prearranged to enable Chicago to catch a train to Boston, would have ended the game. Dick Williams was at bat, with lefthander Paul LaPalme pitching for the Sox. All LaPalme had to do was hold the ball, throw it on the screen, in the dirt, anywhere but in the strike zone, and Chicago would have won. Manager Al Lopez even went to the mound to discuss the options with LaPalme.

No sooner had Al returned to the bench than

A MIRACLE ON 33RD ST. ALMOST!....

ORIOLES'
CHRISTMAS CARD.
1960 WORLD SERIES
TICKETS DID NOT
GO UNUSED.

★

RICHARDS AND HIS COACHING STAFF IN
'60: HARRY BRECHEEN, JIMMY ADAIR AND
LUMAN HARRIS.

★

JIM GENTILE CROSSING HOME PLATE AFTER HITTING THE 4TH OF HIS RECORD TYING 5 GRAND SLAMS IN '61...THAT YEAR "DIAMOND JIM" HIT A TOTAL OF 46 HOMERS, DROVE IN 141 RUNS AND BATTED .302. HERE HE'S CONGRATULATED BY RON HANSEN, HANK FOILES AND WHITEY HERZOG. THE KANSAS CITY A'S CATCHER IS JOE PIGNATANO AND THE UMPIRE JOHN FLAHERTY.

★

LaPalme threw a strike and Williams hit a home run, tying the score, with time expiring as he rounded the bases. Lopez was still in shock in the clubhouse as he dressed for the train trip. The game had to be replayed in its entirety later, and to add insult to injury the Orioles won the replay.

Between June 24-28 that season, four veteran Orioles tied a league record by pitching consecutive shutouts, all in Memorial Stadium. Skinny Brown started it by blanking the Tigers 6-0. The next day, Billy Loes shutout the Kansas City Athletics, 5-0. Connie Johnson stopped the A's, 1-0, and Ray Moore finished the streak, beating Cleveland 6-0. The next two seasons the club slipped back below .500, but there was ever increasing evidence that the farm system was close to being ready to help at the major league level. Even so, 1958 and '59 were far from dull.

For one thing, the Orioles hosted their first, and only, All-Star Game in 1958, and Billy O'Dell was the MVP. Casey Stengel brought in "The Digger" in the 7th inning to protect a 4-3 American League lead, and the little Orioles' lefthander retired all nine men in order on 27 pitches.

On Sep 20 of that year, Hoyt Wilhelm pitched the first no-hitter in Orioles' modern history, beating the Yankees, 1-0, on a home run by Triandos. For big Gus, who was the Orioles MVP that year, it was his 30th homer, tying him with Yogi Berra for the most hit by a catcher in one season to that time. What is forgotten now is that Triandos hit another home run earlier that year in Detroit, but it was nullified when the game was rained out.

Another memorable game that season, the night before the no-hitter, came against the Yankees

THE ORIOLES PITCHING STAFF IN THE LATE 50S & EARLY 60S WAS A MIXTURE OF YOUTH AND EXPERIENCE (L TO R): HAL BROWN, MILT PAPPAS, HOYT WILHELM, JERRY WALKER AND JACK FISHER.

★

Orioles-Yankees Box

NEW YORK	Ab	R	H	Rbi	E		ORIOLES	Ab	R	H	Rbi	E
Bauer, rf	4	0	0	0	0		Williams, 3b-lf	4	0	1	0	0
Lumpe, ss	2	0	0	0	0		Boyd, 1b	2	0	0	0	0
Mantle, cf	3	0	0	0	0		Woodling, rf	1	0	1	0	0
Skowron, 3b	3	0	0	0	2		Busby, cf	3	0	0	0	0
Siebern, lf	3	0	0	0	0		Nieman, lf	1	0	1	1	0
Howard, c	2	0	0	0	0		Robinson, 3b	3	1	1	0	0
Throneberry, 1b	1	0	0	0	0		Triandos, c	3	0	0	0	0
1Berra, 1b	2	0	0	0	0		Tasby, cf-rf	3	0	1	0	0
Richardson, 2b	0	0	0	0	0		Gardner, 2b	2	0	0	0	0
Shantz, p	1	0	0	0	0		Castleman, ss	0	0	0	0	0
2Slaughter	1	0	0	0	0		Miranda, ss	3	0	0	0	0
							Wilhelm, p					
Totals	26	0	0	0	2		Totals	29	1	5	1	0

1Grounded out for Throneberry in ninth.
1Grounded out for Throneberry in eighth; 2Flied out for Shantz in

New York .... 0 0 0 0 0 0 0 0 0 0—0
ORIOLES .... 0 0 0 0 0 0 1 0 x—1

Putouts and assists—New York, 24-5; ORIOLES, 27—7. Left on bases —New York, 1; ORIOLES, 6. Two-base hit—Williams. Home run—Triandos. Passed ball—Triandos.

PITCHING RECORD

	Ip	H	R	Er	Bb	So		Ip	H	R	Er	Bb	So
Wilhelm (W., 3-10)	9	0	0	0	2	8	Shantz (L., 7-6)	2	4	1	1	0	2
Larsen	6	1	0	0	2	2							

Umpires—Paparella, Chylak, Tabacchi and Stuart. Time—1.48. Attendance—16,941.

when the Orioles, trailing, 4-0, in the 9th, produced 5 runs, the tying and winning runs scoring on a single by Woodling.

After the '58 season, Lee MacPhail was hired to replace Richards as general manager, with Paul continuing as manager. It was a good move. Richards had laid the foundation, but the front office was in need of some streamlining and reorganization and MacPhail was the right man for the job. The change also gave Paul an opportunity to concentrate on managing.

It is my opinion that MacPhail was one of the most underrated executives in Orioles history, a man who did much to take the team from where it was when he arrived to that first World Championship in 1966.

In 1959, the Orioles and White Sox played an incredible season series. Since both featured good pitching and defense, and were a little light offensively, their games went on seemingly forever. In those days every club played 22 games against each opponent. That year, the O's and White Sox played the equivalent of 27, five extra games. They had one 18-inning game, two of 17 innings, one of 16, two of 10.

On May 19 that year, O'Dell won his own game with a home run that traveled only 120 feet in the air, and produced both runs in a 2-1 victory over Billy Pierce and the White Sox. The looping pop-up carried just beyond first base, landed on the foul line, which was made of wood painted white (and still is), bounced over the head of onrushing rightfielder Al Smith, and before he could retrieve it, O'Dell had rounded the bases.

Hoyt Wilhelm, now a Hall of Famer primarily as a relief pitcher, made history in '59, winning nine in a row at the start, when Richards used him as a

WILLIE MAYS AWAITS 1ST PITCH OF THE '58 ALL-STAR GAME FROM BOB TURLEY,
THEN WITH THE YANKEES. TURLEY, OF COURSE, ALSO HAD THE DISTINCTION OF
STARTING THE 1ST GAME EVER PLAYED AT MEMORIAL STADIUM, IN '54.

★

starter. On May 22 and 28, in successive starts against the Yankees, he pitched one-hit and four-hit shutouts, winning both games 5-0. In six starts against the Bronx Bombers starting with the no-hitter the previous September, Hoyt had gone 5-0 with 5 complete games, and had allowed only 3 earned runs and 19 hits in 52 innings vs New York's finest.

Those who were in Memorial Stadium on June 10 that season will never forget it, because they saw Cleveland's Rocky Colavito hit four consecutive home runs, one longer than the other, tying a big league record in an 11-8 Indians victory.

July 9 was a memorable date on several counts. First, two 20-year-olds, Milt Pappas and Jerry Walker, shut out the Senators in both ends of a doubleheader. And even more significant, it was also the day a third baseman by the name of Brooks Robinson returned from the minor leagues to stay.

On Sep 11, 20-year-old pitchers again hurled shutouts in a doubleheader, this time against the soon to be American League champion White Sox. Jack Fisher won the first game, 3-0, then Walker came back to pitch 16 scoreless innings before winning on a "sudden death" single by Brooks that produced the game's only run. The farm system was obviously making its presence felt.

In 1960, with Jim Gentile picked up out of the Dodgers organization, where he had been stymied behind Gil Hodges, the Orioles had an infield that produced both offensively and defensively, with Gentile at first, Marv Breeding at second, Ron Hansen at short, and Robinson at third. Triandos did most of the catching, backed up by Clint Courtney. Jack Brandt, Woodling, and Al Pilarcik were the outfield regulars supported by Jim Busby and Gene Stephens, and with a pitching staff comprising Kiddie Korps members Chuck Estrada, Pappas, Fisher, Walker and Steve Barber, and veterans Skinny Brown, and Wilhelm, the Orioles were ready to make a run at the Yankees. There were seven rookies and 10 front liners in their 20s on that 1960 club that almost brought the Orioles their first pennant.

★
HOYT WILHELM'S NO-HITTER
AGAINST THE YANKEES IN SEP '58
STILL RANKS AMONG THE BEST OF
ORIOLES HIGHLIGHTS. HERE HE'S
CONGRATULATED BY TEAMMATES
AND AN UNIDENTIFIED
GROUNDSKEEPER (L TO R): EDDIE
ROBINSON, MILT PAPPAS, FOSTER
CASTLEMAN, DICK WILLIAMS,
(FACE OBSCURED BY
GROUNDSKEEPER), JOE GINSBERG,
ARNIE PORTOCARRERO AND BILLY
LOES.

TED KLUSZEWSKI'S "HOME RUN"
THAT WAS NULLIFIED BECAUSE TIME HAD BEEN CALLED JUST BEFORE
MILT PAPPAS HAD DELIVERED THE PITCH...BIG KLU REACHED 3RD
BASE BEFORE HE GOT THE WORD THAT WHAT WAS PROBABLY A GAME-
WINNING HOMER DIDN'T COUNT, AND HE'D HAVE TO GO BACK AND BAT
AGAIN. LOWER RIGHT, WHITE SOX MANAGER AL LOPEZ ARGUES WITH
3RD BASE UMPIRE ED HURLEY WHO HAD MADE THE TIMEOUT CALL.
THE ORIOLES 3RD BASEMAN IS UNIDENTIFIED.

On Sep 4, after sweeping a 3-game series against the Yankees, in Baltimore, they led the league by two games, and they were still in a virtual tie with the Yankees on the 15th when they moved into Yankee Stadium for a crucial four-game series.

Going down the stretch with a chance to win it all was a first for the Orioles, but old hat for the Yankees, who had been through it all for so many years. The Yankees won them all, then cruised to the pennant eight games in front of the Birds, who wound up second with a record of 89-65.

It was during that season that the Orioles unveiled the "big mitt," an out-sized catcher's glove designed by Richards to enable Triandos and Courtney to better box Wilhelm's fluttering and evasive knuckler. After watching Courtney circle under a high pop fly seemingly forever in Yankee Stadium, a New York reporter wrote that "Old Scraps" looked for all the world like a waiter carrying a big tray of pizzas.

A strange thing happened on Aug 28 that season. The Orioles were leading the White Sox, 3-1, in the 8th at Memorial Stadium, when Big Ted Kluszewski hit a three-run homer off Pappas. However, Ed Hurley, the umpire at third base, had called time just before the pitch was delivered because Earl Torgeson and Floyd Robinson, preparing to enter the game defensively the next inning, were warming up outside the prescribed bullpen area (in those days the bullpens were down the left and right field foul lines). The Sox argued long and loud, but Hurley stood firm, the "homer" was erased, and the Orioles went on to win 3-1.

That series against the Yankees, Sep. 2-4, was about as exciting as any the Orioles had played since getting into the league. Before 114,000, the Orioles won all three games to take a two-game lead. On Friday night, Pappas beat Whitey Ford, 5-0, on three hits. Saturday, Fisher shut them out 2-0, on seven hits, with Brooks Robinson knocking in both runs. Then, on Sunday, Estrada and Wilhelm combined on a 7-2 victory. Estrada had a no-hitter until Bill Skowron singled with two out in the 7th as the Yanks scored twice, ending a string of 25 scoreless innings.

ROGER MARIS SCORING AFTER HITTING HIS 59TH HOME RUN OF THE YEAR, OFF MILT PAPPAS IN SEP '61...NO ONE OTHER THAN BABE RUTH HAD EVER HIT MORE THAN 58 HOMERS IN ONE SEASON...MARIS, OF COURSE, FINISHED WITH A RECORD 61 HOMERS AND ALSO LED THE LEAGUE IN RBI WITH 142, JUST ONE MORE THAN JIM GENTILE...THAT'S YOGI BERRA CONGRATULATING MARIS.

★

LEE MACPHAIL REPLACED RICHARDS AS GENERAL MANAGER AFTER THE '58 SEASON, BUT PAUL REMAINED AS FIELD MANAGER.

★

In 1961, which was Richards's final year, the Orioles won more games to finish at 95-67, yet were never really a threat, finishing third, 13 1/2 games behind the all-powerful Yankees, who won 109, and the Tigers, with 101.

It was an expansion year, a year dominated by explosive batting performances. Gentile provided the fireworks for the Orioles with arguably the best offensive year ever put together by an Oriole.

"Diamond Jim" became the first player in major league history to hit grand slam home runs in successive at bats in the same game, on May 9 in Minnesota. For the year, Gentile had five grand slams, an American League record, tying the major league mark of Ernie Banks.

Even though he hit .302, with 46 home runs and 141 runs batted in, Gentile led the league in nothing, because that was the year Maris hit 61 homers for the all-time record, and Mickey Mantle hit 54. Maris edged Gentile for the rbi title 142 to 141. Because he wanted to hit over .300, Gentile sat out the final game of the season.

When he was asked later why he didn't try to beat out Maris for the rbi title the year the Yankee broke Babe Ruth's home run record, he acknowledged he probably should have, but didn't think of it at the time.

On the morning of Aug 30, with the team in Los Angeles to play the Angels that night, Richards called and asked me to come to his room. He said he had decided to resign to become general manager of Houston and said he would like me to write the story. He said it originally was to have been announced at the end of the season, but he didn't believe it could be kept secret that long. It surprised me, because there had been no rumors.

He explained that unless he won a pennant, about 7-8 years was the maximum a manager should stay in one place, and that anyway, at this stage of his career, it was probably best for him to get off the field and into the front office. Also, he couldn't turn down an offer to return to his beloved state of Texas as general manager.

He had served the Orioles well. The team on the field was ready to compete with the best, the farm system producing, and the front office staffed to carry everything forward. The Richards era did not

produce a pennant, but it set the stage. The Orioles were the winningest team in the majors over the next 30 years or so, and Paul Richards played a huge role in that success.

Later, after he'd mellowed a bit, this tall, taciturn Texan, "Number 12" as he was frequently called, would freely admit, as to how Baltimore and the Orioles had meant a lot to him, too.

ALL IN ALL, BALTIMORE'S BASEBALL FORTUNES IMPROVED MARKEDLY UNDER RICHARDS' TUTELAGE. HERE YANKEES MANAGER CASEY STENGEL WITH ELLIE HOWARD AND TWO UNIDENTIFIED PLAYERS LOOK ON GLUMLY AS THE ORIOLES PUT THE GAME OUT OF REACH...THAT BECAME A FAMILIAR SCENE IN ENEMY DUGOUTS DURING THE NEXT 30 YEARS OR SO.

★

MANY SAY TED WILLIAMS WAS THE BEST HITTER IN BASEBALL HISTORY, AND THAT WOULD BE TOUGH TO ARGUE. BUT HERE THE O'S GOT HIM ON STRIKES. GUS TRIANDOS WAS THE CATCHER, AND THE PITCHER ARNIE PORTOCARRERO.

★

Taming the Monster

BY JIM BREADY

Memorial Stadium in its photos stands there large, colorful, full of memories—and unmoving. People in the future who were never there for Orioles games are going to think of it as a lovely place, but always the same. How wrong of them.

If you were a 1991 stadium-goer, but young, you should've been there when the upper-deck seating was wood benches. A posterior could get stabbed, on those benches—and often did. If you go back a way, do you remember the dugouts before they were reversed—when the Orioles were on the first base side, the enemy on third?

In 1954, this was the newest, grandest ballpark in Organized Baseball. But not for long—stadium-building was in vogue nationwide. Striving to keep up, the City of Baltimore, as the owner of Memorial Stadium, improved or modernized some facet (chiefly during the off season) almost every year after 1954. That year itself, the emphasis had been on simple

A TOUGH TICKET TO FIND...OPENING DAY '54.

★

completion—while the 46,354 ticket buyers who flooded in on April 15, Opening Day, noticed empty places in the exterior bricking, nonetheless they found the promenades navigable, the johns flushable, the paint on the seats dry. To get to and from the upper decks, many walked eight flights of concrete ramp.

Three major structural changes occurred: First, in 1961, the insertion of field-edge boxes, lowering the 8-foot wall that had distanced the fans from the players, and shrinking a foul ground that had bedeviled fielders and batters alike; second, in 1964, the lengthening of the upper deck, two sections being added at either end of the horseshoe, and the installation there of escalators; third, in 1985, the exterior modification that added to the number of fan rest rooms and meant more office space for the Orioles' long-cramped management. (Then the front office could be truly out in front, with actual windows in some of the rooms, instead of in cells or catacombs under the stands.)

Meanwhile, metal benches replaced wood, and seats or chair backs were installed in the upper deck. The press box and its restaurant-lounge underwent several renovations. Alongside, there on the mezzanine, the closing in of several sections to make an owner's box, a Designated Hitters' box, additional broadcasting boxes and several corporation-rental sky boxes, over the years, also constituted significant change. In the process, total capacity rose from about 46,500 to 54,017 (the view from 3,484 lower-deck seats partially obstructed by support pillars).

Dating an aerial photo of Memorial Stadium and its parking lot isn't always easy. If there are few buses at rest in the southwest corner, the picture goes back a bit. If a football grid shows across the diamond, it is probably a pre-1983 autumn. The single largest clue is the scoreboard. Its figures and wording can be helpful indeed. The topic is tame now, in an age of advertiser diversity; but Baltimore's long overdue re-entry into the major leagues, back there in 1954, meant high noon in the beer wars. Behind the scenes, Highlandtown's two big breweries slugged it out for fan attention. That first year, Gunther had the scoreboard all to itself with a Longines clock above it; National had the broadcasting rights all to itself.

MASTER CONTROL: EARLE MURPHY (TOP) ON BALLS AND STRIKES AND HIS PARTNER AL GERNAT, AT THE OUT-OF-TOWN SCORES PANEL.

★

THE ORIGINAL SCOREBOARD...SCORES FROM OTHER GAMES AND THE CORRECT TIME, TOO.

★

THE "NEW" SCOREBOARD, ERECTED IN '70, NOW KNOWN
AS THE "OLD" SCOREBOARD.

★

IN THE BACKGROUND, ACROSS 36TH STREET, THE
INFAMOUS "WHITE HOUSES." HARD ON THE HITTERS.

★

Eventually, Gunther obtained the TV and radio rights too—only to relinquish everything when the firm was sold and shut down. An ad for Hamm's, an out-of-town beer, briefly dominated the scoreboard. Then National, buying heavily into Orioles stock, monopolized the scene. Meanwhile, the 65-foot high scoreboard, a point of pride in 1954, was growing obsolete. Two employees had to be at their places inside, operating it; and squirrels loved it,

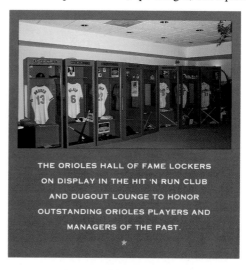

THE ORIOLES HALL OF FAME LOCKERS
ON DISPLAY IN THE HIT 'N RUN CLUB
AND DUGOUT LOUNGE TO HONOR
OUTSTANDING ORIOLES PLAYERS AND
MANAGERS OF THE PAST.

★

nesting inside and chewing on the wires. Still, scores could be posted for all games underway elsewhere. In other cities, newer scoreboards were remote-controlled, from the press box; they could in an instant replace the scoring with verbal messages—saying hello, for instance, to a group of fans from any locality or organization— and then go back to the game. Some scoreboards were equipped to perform tricks, e.g., Chicago A.L.'s, which would set off fireworks in response to a White Sox home run.

THE STATE-OF-THE-ART
DIAMOND VISION
VIDEO BOARD BY
MITSUBISHI, UNDER
CONSTRUCTION IN '85,
PROVIDES INFORMA-
TION AND PICTURES
NOT EVEN DREAMED
OF WHEN THE BALL
PARK WAS BUILT 31
YEARS EARLIER.

★

In 1970, Baltimore took down the outdated scoreboard, replacing it with a smaller one that could, however, double as a message board. It could also, in alternation, accommodate a variety of advertisers. Occasionally a glitch occurred, digital or electrical, and viewers could pounce on typographical errors. In 1985, an additional picture board went up in right-center: Diamond Vision, replays and between-innings entertainment.

Concessions changed markedly—not just the inevitable upward drift of parking, beer and hot dog prices, but the broadening of the promenade food stands' bill of fare to include such undreamed of (in 1954) delights as crab cakes, knishes and guacamole. Overhead TV screens enabled patrons waiting in line to keep up with the field action meantime. For those who arrived early, a ground-level, full-scale restaurant, the Hit and Run Club, was also added, to serve full, regular lunch or dinner; patrons could gawk at the simulated lockers of players who had been elected to the Orioles Hall of Fame.

In other ways, the promenades changed from open-air corridors to shopping malls. The Orioles' logo appeared on a staggering multiplicity of manufactured souvenirs, on all manner of things to wear, use, read, or simply collect. This process was stimulated by intermittent advertiser freebies, these often being useful objects; from 1960 on, the Oriole Advocates took their stations at the entry gates, politely presenting a given day's giveaway. At any other points on upper or lower promenade, it became possible to gauge one's throwing speed, to have one's photo taken with an Orioles player in cutout, to sign up for season tickets next year.

(An aside on tickets: A collector would report great variation during Memorial Stadium's history. The high points are of course the fancy paintings for 1958's All-Star Game and the 1966, 1969, 1970, 1971, 1979, and 1983 World Series; the low points, either today's computer printouts or, all the way back to the start, the original opening day, when management passed up the chance to issue something appropriately commemorative. Today,

THE TOWER OF PIZZA:
AN INNOVATIVE IDEA
IN 1970.

⭑

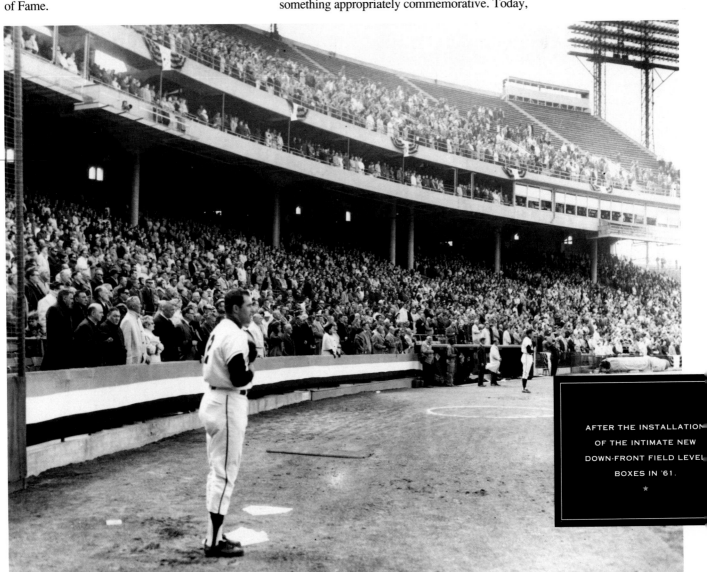

AFTER THE INSTALLATION
OF THE INTIMATE NEW
DOWN-FRONT FIELD LEVEL
BOXES IN '61.

⭑

ironically, no drab, full, untorn April 15, 1954, ticket seems to exist.)

The changes in home-team and visitor club-houses reflected improvements in the care and conditioning of athletes generally. In 1954, players still sought off-season, often sit-down, jobs. With higher contract salaries, they have the free time necessary for remaining in shape year-round. Indoor batting and throwing cages have come into use throughout the majors, since 1954. The feature that particularly fetched civilians, as an expanded Orioles public affairs section undertook occasional guided tours, was the weight room with its advanced apparatus.

By and large, however, when fans were testing one another's baseball acumen, their challenges most often related to aspect of the playing surface. The original outfield, more like a prairie, that so dismayed Gil Coan, the first Orioles centerfielder—in what four years was it reduced from 450 feet straightaway to the final 405 feet? (In 154-game 1954, the highest number of home runs by an Oriole

THE BROKEN LINE ILLUSTRATES THE TWO NEW UPPER DECK SECTIONS WHEN THEY WERE ADDED TO THE LEFTFIELD END OF THE HORSESHOE IN '64...TWO SECTIONS WERE ALSO BUILT IN RIGHTFIELD AT THE SAME TIME.

HE ORIGINAL FRONT ROW OX SEATS, A LONG WAY FROM THE ACTION.

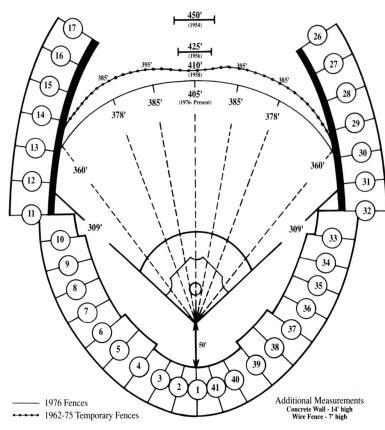

450'
(1954)

425'
(1956)

395'   410'   395'
(1958)

385'   385'

405'
385'   (1976- Present)   385'

378'   378'

360'   360'

309'   309'

50'

——— 1976 Fences

•••••• 1962-75 Temporary Fences

Additional Measurements
Concrete Wall - 14' high
Wire Fence - 7' high

*The distance to the fence in straightaway center field has been 410' since 1958. However,
the distances in left and right center were reduced in 1962.

★

BRINGING IN THE FENCES IN STAGES, OR "GIVING THE
HITTER AN EVEN BREAK."

was 8—the same maximum as hit by another Oriole in the 138-game season of 1902. Until the shrinking, Memorial Stadium produced the most home runs of any major league park.) When did Chuck Diering take away a homer from Mickey Mantle by spearing the ball as he tumbled into the hedge? When was the fence installed, for Mickey Mantle to break his ankle in? When was the fence padded? When did the custom of tomato-plant corner begin? In what different vehicles have relief pitchers been driven in from the bullpens? When was the HERE sign first raised at the back edge of the left field bleachers? When were the other-city perimeter flags added? How many seats were added when a World Series was about to be played? What legends were painted, over the years, on the dugout roofs? What were the irreverent words that trespassers once burned into the infield grass?

Go to a ballpark every summer for 38 years and what you see, on closing your eyes, isn't just the structural outlines, inside and out. You see it now looking one way, now looking a dozen other ways. But mainly, in its phantasmagory (ed: an illusory mental image as in a dream) of visual aspects, Memorial Stadium abides.

A BLEND OF OLD AND NEW. THE INSPIRATION FOR FIELD BOX
SEATS, PERMANENTLY ADDED IN '61, WAS PROVIDED BY THE
TEMPORARY FIELD SEATS CONSTRUCTED THREE YEARS EARLIER TO
ACCOMMODATE AN OVERFLOW CROWD FOR THE '58 ALL-STAR GAME.

★

Just BEFORE Dawn

BY BOB BROWN

Though the first four years after Richards departure didn't bring any pennants to Baltimore, they were certainly not wasted.

To the contrary, the Orioles farm system was never so fertile as it was in the early sixties, and, during those four seasons from '62 thru '65, many of the players that would contribute significantly to making the Orioles a dominant team in the upcoming era served their apprenticeships—either in the high minors or at the big league level, or both.

In no particular order these future Orioles standouts included: Boog Powell, Dave McNally, Andy Etchebarren, Jim Palmer, Dave Johnson, Paul Blair, Curt Motton, Eddie Watt, Mark Belanger, Tom Phoebus, Wally Bunker and Curt Blefary.

The Orioles' minor league organization, which had first achieved prominence in the 50s under the guidance of Richards and farm director Jim McLaughlin, embellished its reputation further in the 60s with Harry Dalton and his boss Lee MacPhail in control.

AFFABLE BILLY HITCHCOCK, PICTURED HERE WITH GENERAL MANAGER LEE MACPHAIL, REPLACED PAUL RICHARDS AS MANAGER IN '62.

In the final month of the '62 season, the Orioles had 33 players in uniform, 20 of them from the farm system. Over a two year stretch ('63 & '64),

THE O'S THREE BIG WINNERS IN '64: WALLY BUNKER, HANK BAUER, AND BROOKS ROBINSON.

every one of the Orioles six minor league clubs won at least one pennant and/or league playoff, and in '62 alone, 15 Orioles farmhands were chosen to league all-star teams.

Billy Hitchcock, the affable gentlemen from Opelika, Alabama, succeeded Richards as manager in '62, then two years later the equally personable Hank Bauer replaced Billy.

It was also during that time that the Orioles made an important deal with the White Sox, that brought to Baltimore one of baseball's all-time greatest shortstops, Hall of Famer Luis Aparicio. He would prove to be an immense contributor over the next several years, with his bat, his legs and his glove and along with infield partners Brooks Robinson and Jerry Adair (later Dave Johnson) did much to establish the Orioles' reputation for defensive excellence.

The Birds did almost win their first pennant, in '64, but just as they had in '60, fell short at the end. The fact is they won 97 games that year to

finish 3rd, 2 games out. Two seasons later, they would win 97 games again and capture the pennant by 9 games. How do you figure it?

There were some marvelous moments in '64, the year three Orioles captured major awards. Brooks was the "mvp," Hank Bauer "manager of the year" and Wally Bunker "rookie pitcher of the year."

One very dramatic Orioles success that summer had a song written about it. It was called "That Yankee Game," and was just one number in an entire musical score, composed by Baltimore ad man Bobby Goodman about the '64 Orioles, entitled "Pennant Fever."

"That Yankee Game" was played on June 23 and there wasn't much to write about for the first 7 1/2 innings. The Orioles came to bat in the bottom of the 8th trailing the vaunted Yankees (who would win their 5th straight AL championship that year) by 7-2. Then with two out, the Birds came battling back, scored 7 times, and went ahead 9-7. Jerry Adair drove in the tie-breaker, and Charlie Lau singled and doubled while pinch-hitting twice in the big inning. Roger Maris hit a solo home run for the Bombers in the 9th to make it closer, but the Orioles held on to win.

When the Birds took the field for the top of the 9th, 31,000 Orioles fans/Yankee haters were delirious as they stood in unison and cheered them

SKINNY BOOG POWELL DURING THE EARLY 60S.

A TRIO OF ALL-TIME GREATS: OUR OWN CHUCK THOMPSON AND TWO HALL OF FAMERS, JACKIE ROBINSON AND BOB FELLER, AT MEMORIAL STADIUM IN '64.

IN '63 STEVE BARBER BECAME THE FIRST MAJOR LEAGUE ORIOLE TO WIN 20-GAMES IN 62 SEASONS.

wildly. No one on the club at the time could remember ever getting a standing ovation before. There have been a lot of them since then.

In '62, Billy Hitchcock's first year at the helm, the Orioles finished under .500, 18 games off their '61 victory total, but still there were some good times:

Like a five game sweep of the Yankees, who had flown all Thursday night from the West Coast to get here, then dropped a twi-night doubleheader Friday, both ends of a day-night (separate admission) twin bill Saturday and a single game Sunday. The finale, which ended in a 2-1 win for the Orioles, was particularly exciting.

Hall of Famers Robin Roberts and Whitey Ford were tied 1-1 (on early home runs by Brooks and Tony Kubek) until Jim Gentile, whom Ford would strike out three times in four trips that day, homered off the Yankees lefthander in the 4th and the lead held up.

A month later Dave McNally and Andy Etchebarren, Elmira Pioneer's manager Earl

Weaver's prize battery that season, made their big league debuts as an entry at the stadium, against the Kansas City A's. Mac blanked them on two hits and Andy singled in a run in his first big league at bat.

In '63 the Orioles jumped out to a 30-15 start, but swooned in June and finished well out of the money, though they did win a respectable 86 games.

Steve Barber, that season, became the first major league Oriole to win 20 since Joe McGinnity went 26-20 for John McGraw's AL Orioles of '01; Stu Miller won the first of his two most valuable Oriole awards, and Boog Powell began to emerge as a star of the future.

After the near miss of '64, the Orioles never seriously contended in '65, but they still won 94 games, and now the pieces were almost in place; the good times were about to roll.

1 9 6 6

Would You Believe Four Straight?

BY GORDON BEARD

The Orioles' franchise came of age on Oct 9, 1966, 10 months to the day after Frank Robinson was acquired in a trade that turned a team of sometimes pretenders into perennial contenders.

It was on that date that the Orioles completed their incredible four-game sweep of the heavily favored Los Angeles Dodgers to nail down their first World Series championship.

Suddenly, the tantalizing, somewhat bitter, near misses of 1960 and 1964 were forgotten by frenzied fans who had waited for this moment since the

Orioles returned to the major leagues in 1954.

Like the Orioles, staid old Baltimore would never be the same, either. The euphoria that accompanied a season of domination by the Orioles ended the city's inferiority complex. The winning feeling seemed to infect the entire populace.

Attendance at Memorial Stadium, though not huge by standards of the late '80s and early '90s, reached a club record 1,203,366 in 1966. The Orioles won 48 of 79 games at home that year, providing many memorable moments along with

CAPTURE THE MOMENT....THE BALTIMORE ORIOLES ARE CHAMPIONS OF THE WORLD.

the victories.

The most notable came before the largest crowd. The feat, which will live in Oriole history and be a favorite topic of trivia buffs long after the final season is played at Memorial Stadium in 1991, came in the second game of a Sunday doubleheader on May 8.

Playing in only his 10th game before his new home fans, since being acquired in a trade with Cincinnati, Frank Robinson became the first player to hit a ball completely out of Memorial Stadium. And, as the 1991 season unfolded, he remained the ONLY one.

Few in attendance that day will ever forget Frank's drive off Cleveland's Luis Tiant sailing over the left field bleachers, near the foul line, or the minute-long standing ovation he received when he took his position in right field at the start of the second inning.

The homer was measured as traveling 451 feet

A GUTSY ORIOLES
ADVERTISING
MANEUVER...THIS
BILLBOARD WENT UP IN
FRONT OF THE STADIUM
THE DAY OF GAME #3,
WELL BEFORE THE SWEEP
WAS OFFICIAL.

★

on the fly before rolling to a stop on the parking lot, 540 feet from home plate.

The official attendance that day was 37,658, but when 11,858 non-paying Safety Patrol youngsters were added to the total, the unofficial count of 49,516 represented the largest turnout in Baltimore's major league history to that point. To commemorate Frank's slugging feat, on May 19, the Oriole Advocates, a group which promotes and stimulates interest in baseball, raised a flag at the railing where the home run left the park. The banner was inscribed, simply: "HERE."

Pitcher Milt Pappas, the principal figure in the 3-for-1 trade for Frank, had predicted the newest Oriole would have more trouble hitting homers in Memorial Stadium than in Cincinnati's bandbox Crosley Field, where he played for 10 seasons.

Frank's pre-season response to the Pappas statement was, "The ball will go out anywhere if you hit it right." Proving his point, he hit 27 of his career-high 49 homers in Memorial Stadium, and by adding 122 runs batted in and a .316 batting average, became a Triple Crown winner. He homered in the season opener before the home fans. Shortly after the All-Star break, Frank led the O's in beating back a mild challenge from Detroit. In a sweep at home over the Tigers, July 19-21, he had nine hits, including four homers, drove in eight runs and scored six.

Brooks Robinson, who admitted to being spurred to greater heights by the presence of Frank, drove home 18 runs in the first 10 games and had 70 by midseason before a prolonged slump

The Deal

by Harry Dalton

Lee MacPhail is the one who did almost all the work on the Frank Robinson trade. He was still the general manager at the time and had just made a deal with the Phillies a week before. He had picked up a reliever named Jack Baldschun and Dick Simpson, an outfielder.

He was also talking with Cincinnati about getting Frank Robinson, and they had a deal in place involving Milt Pappas, Baldschun and Simpson for Frank. That was just at the time Lee was leaving to go to the Commissioner's Office, and I was taking over as general manager.

On the morning of the press conference announcing the administrative changes, Lee came into my office with a sheet of paper and said, "Here's your first decision." On it were the four names- Robinson, Pappas, Simpson and Baldschun. He said, "Bill DeWitt (the Reds' gm) is interested in doing this and it's up to you to decide whether or not you want to do it." With that, we went right into the press conference.

It wasn't until later in the day that we had a chance to sit down and talk about it in detail. Actually I never really had any doubt about wanting to do it. The one thing I tried to do, since we were giving them three players, was to get an additional player from Cincinnati, a young prospect.

I talked to Bill DeWitt for about 24 hours on that trying to get a young lefthanded pitcher they had. He said, no he wouldn't do that. The only pitcher he'd consider was Roger Craig (now manager of the San Francisco Giants), but at that point we felt Craig's career was pretty well behind him.

We turned that down, and without waiting any longer decided to make the deal.

EXECUTIVE VICE-PRESIDENT FRANK CASHEN AND
GENERAL MANAGER HARRY DALTON HAD GREAT
ROOKIE SEASONS IN THEIR NEW POSITIONS IN '66.

★

limited his year-end total to 100.

Boog Powell, who finished second in the league with 109 rbi and third with 34 homers despite hitting only one homer over the final six weeks because of a chip fracture of his left ring finger, had his biggest day on July 6.

In a twi-night doubleheader at home against Kansas City, Boog tied an American League record with 11 rbi. He hit two homers and two doubles. One homer was a grand slam, and he narrowly missed another on a sacrifice fly hauled down at the fence.

But there was more, much more, for the home fans to enjoy in one of the most memorable of the 38 seasons the Orioles were to play in Memorial Stadium:

—Frank, Brooks and Boog finished 1-2-3 in the A.L. "mvp" vote that winter, and shortstop Louie Aparicio was 9th.

—Billy Short, just recalled from Rochester, recorded his first victory in six years, a 2-0 shutout on July 1, during a five-game sweep of the defending American League champion Minnesota Twins.

MANAGER HANK BAUER, SHAVING FOR THE VICTORY PARTY, HUGS HIS ACE LEFTHANDER DAVE MCNALLY AFTER MAC'S TITLE CLINCHING 4-HIT 1-0 SHUTOUT.

★

THEY STILL CALL HIM "CAKES"—JIM PALMER EARNED HIS NICKNAME IN '66 WHEN HE INSISTED ON EATING PANCAKES FOR BREAKFAST ON THE DAYS HE WAS TO PITCH.

★

—Jim Palmer, the club's biggest winner at 15-10, beat Chicago on July 22 and then revealed that he had won seven of his last eight decisions after eating pancakes for breakfast on game day.

His lone loss came during that span had come on June 28, after he had gulped down only a muffin and half a grapefruit in his haste to catch a team plane that morning. To this day, Palmer is still known to old friends as "Cakes."

—Homegrown pitcher Tom Phoebus, only the sixth pitcher since 1900 to toss shutouts in his first two major league starts, notched the first at home on Sep

15, with his mother, brother and 14 other relatives in the stands.

The Orioles were given permission on Sep 8 to print World Series tickets. This time, they didn't wind up as novel Christmas cards, as they had after the near miss of 1960. And, they weren't burned, which was the fate of unused 1964 tickets.

The record book shows the pennant was clinched with a victory at Kansas City on Sep 22, but those who believe in fate would suggest Aug. 22 is a more appropriate date for Oriole fans to celebrate.

On that night, rookie Andy Etchebarren may have saved the life of Frank Robinson, who was foundering in a pool at a private party for the players—at the

ROOKIE CATCHER ANDY ETCHEBARREN WAS CHOSEN TO THE AL ALL-STAR TEAM IN '66 AND CAUGHT EVERY INNING OF ALL FOUR GAMES IN THE WORLD SERIES. BUT, HIS BIGGEST CONTRIBUTION THAT YEAR WAS FISHING FRANK ROBINSON OUT OF THE POOL AT A PARTY FOR THE PLAYERS.

★

home of a funeral director, no less.

Frank, who can't swim, put on a pair of trunks and went into the shallow end of the pool to placate teammates who had threatened to toss him in fully clothed.

But, while jumping around, Frank slipped into the deep end, and went under. Because of his capacity for making jokes, however, his pleas for help went unheeded. His wife, Barbara, knew he couldn't swim, but she also thought Frank was only kidding.

After Frank went down three times, Etchebarren finally jumped in and brought Frank to safety.

The Orioles won the first two games of the World Series in Los Angeles and, with the Dodgers reeling, the action shifted to Baltimore. When the Orioles landed at Friendship International Airport (now BWI) at 1:17 a.m. on Friday, Oct. 7, the welcoming crowd of 9,000 included a fan carrying a sign which read: "Lose just one. I've got tickets to Monday's game."

It was an inventive plea, but it didn't work.

In game No. 3 on Saturday, 21-year-old Wally Bunker, who had only three complete games all season, pitched his first shutout of the year. The game's only run came on a homer by 22-year-old Paul Blair, who had hit just five during the season. Blair was the lone Oriole to advance beyond first base.

FRANK'S 4TH INNING HOME RUN OFF THE DODGERS' DON DRYSDALE PRODUCED THE GAME'S ONLY RUN IN THE DECISIVE 4TH GAME OF THE ORIOLES' SWEEP.

★

PAUL BLAIR HELPED MAKE THE SWEEP POSSIBLE WHEN HE LEAPED HIGH TO CATCH JIM LEFEBVRE'S WOULD-BE HOME RUN IN THE 8TH INNING OF THAT 4TH GAME.

★

As gleeful fans exited Memorial Stadium, they encountered a mobile signboard that had been wheeled onto the median grass plot on 33rd Street. It's succinct message read: "Would you believe four straight?"

On Sunday afternoon, Frank Robinson made believers of the readers. He ended the scoring the way he started it in Los Angeles, with a fourth inning homer that gave 23-year-old Dave McNally a 1-0 victory and extended the scoreless streak of the Dodgers through 33 innings. Paul Blair contributed mightily to the extension of that streak when he stole a home run away from Jim Lefebvre in centerfield during the 8th inning.

A tumultuous celebration spread from Memorial Stadium throughout the city, lasting well into the next morning. When celebrants moved in on a vegetable truck, police were pelted with avocados and artichokes.

That prompted one observer to suggest that, "Baltimoreans have class. In another town, it would have been tomatoes."

As part of the celebration, the City Hall clock was struck 66 times to note that '66 was indeed a very good year.

On opening day of the 1967 season, the championship flag was raised, the first of many that were to adorn the crown of an old friend, venerable Memorial Stadium.

Dynasty
1966-1974

BY GORDON BEARD

No one appreciated the Orioles first championship in 1966 any more than Eddie Weidner, the longtime Orioles trainer and poorman's clubhouse philosopher.

"Don't tell me about 'the good old days,'" said Eddie, who for many years had endured long train rides and inadequate training facilities in the International League. "They weren't even lousy."

But Eddie, who retired after the 1967 season, didn't know that times would get even better for the Orioles and that the 9-year period, 1966-1974, might some day be remembered as "the good old days" of the franchise.

Some baseball observers forecast a dynasty for the Orioles after their sweep of the Los Angeles Dodgers in the 1966 World Series, but Harry Dalton, the club's director of player personnel, tried to keep things in perspective.

"You can't anticipate dynasties,"

THE 1970 ORIOLES
RECORD JACKET BY
DON SCHNABLY.

★

Harry said. "You can only recognize dynasties after they happen.

"We have a chance for a dynasty if we can put together consecutive championships, or be in the race strongly every year and win more than our share of championships—the way the Yankees, Dodgers and Cardinals have in the past 25 years."

Well, looking back, there seems no doubt that the Orioles of the era were indeed a dynasty. One or two more World Series championships would have strengthened the argument immeasurably; but even so, the Orioles were a dominant factor in those years and the 1969-71 teams, which won 318 games and 3 pennants, rank among the best of all time.

Over 9 glorious seasons, the Orioles won 4 American League championships while finishing first 6 times, and 2 World Series titles. They had an imposing 850-593 record during that period, a winning

★

EX-ORIOLE CURT BLEFARY, WHEN ASKED BY A NEWSPAPER
MAN ABOUT THE ORIOLES, RESPONDED, "HELL, THEY'RE NOT
SUPERMEN." WHEN THE YANKEES CAME TO TOWN A FEW DAYS
LATER, THE BIRDS PROVED HIM WRONG.

percentage of .589, an average of almost 95 wins a season, and were a whopping 139 games better than the runner-up Detroit Tigers in the American League.

Despite the club's phenomenal success, fans did not exactly storm the gates in those days (the season average for that period was under one million). But those who visited Memorial Stadium had a chance of witnessing some of the most unforgettable moments in Orioles' history during their run of glory. Among them:

—The two 1-0 shutouts by young pitchers Wally Bunker and Dave McNally, backed by solo homers by Paul Blair and Frank Robinson, as the Orioles completed their upset sweep over the Los Angeles Dodgers in the 1966 World Series.

—Brooks Robinson's incredible 1970 World Series performance.

—Brooks' equally incredible 3 errors in one inning in a 1971 game.

—Dave McNally's World Series grand slam home run in 1970, thru 1990 still the only one ever hit by a pitcher.

—Frank Robinson's gutty base running (despite leg injuries), which kept the O's alive for a deciding 7th game in the 1971 World Series.

—Frank's monstrous home run of 1966, the first ball ever hit completely out of Memorial Stadium...and, as the 1991 season began, still the only one.

—Winning no-hitters by Tom Phoebus and Jim

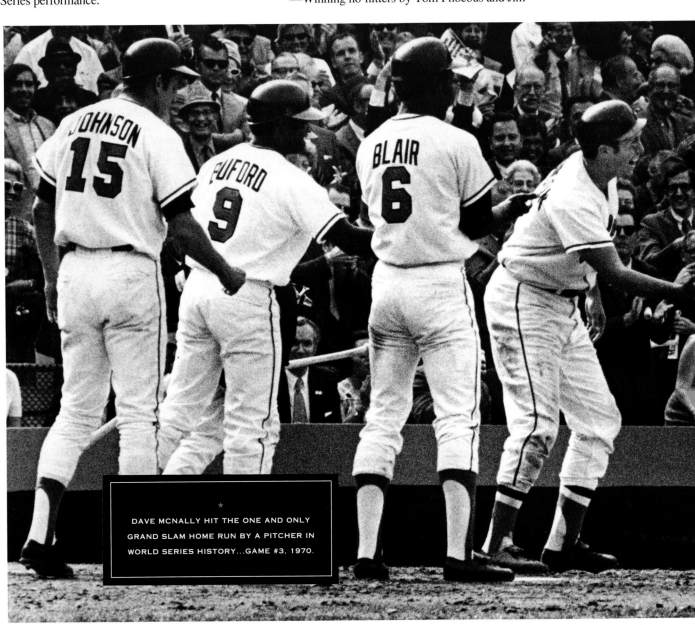

★
DAVE MCNALLY HIT THE ONE AND ONLY
GRAND SLAM HOME RUN BY A PITCHER IN
WORLD SERIES HISTORY...GAME #3, 1970.

FRANK CROSSES HOME PLATE AFTER HIS MILESTONE 500TH HOME RUN LATE ONE NIGHT IN SEP 1971...BOOG OFFERS CON-GRATULATIONS AND BAT- BOY JAY MAZZONE GUARDS THE TREASURED BAT WITH HIS LIFE.

Palmer, and a combined, LOSING no-no by Steve Barber and Stu Miller.

—Boog Powell's record-tying 11 runs batted in during a 1974 doubleheader.

—Milestone hits by Frank, Brooks and Boog.

—An astounding 54-26 domination over the (hated) New York Yankees.

—The longest game in club history (19 innings), the largest margin of victory (17 runs), the most runs in one inning (10), and the smallest crowd at home (655 hardy fans).

To recall pleasant memories for those who were there, or to inform those who weren't, let's relive some of the Memorial Stadium highlights of the "The Dynasty Era."

For Orioles' fans, the 1970 World Series will always be known as the "Brooks Robinson Series."

His spectacular fielding helped the O's win the first two 2 in Cincinnati, prompting teammate Boog Powell to observe on the plane flight to Baltimore: "The Birds dropped some bird seed into the Big Red Machine."

The Reds were indeed psyched. While taking batting practice prior to Game No. 3 in Memorial Stadium, they yelled, "Great play, Brooksie," every

BROOKSIE'S 10TH INNING GRAND SLAM OFF YANKEES' LINDY McDANIEL GIVES O'S A DRAMATIC SUDDEN DEATH VICTORY.

★

time a Cincinnati player hit a grounder to the left side.

Brooks didn't disappoint the home fans, or the Reds. He continued his brilliant fielding as Dave McNally won the third game 9-3, also chipping in with two doubles and two runs batted in. Don Buford and Frank Robinson hit homers, and McNally added his pre-DH slam.

The Reds won the next game, but Mike Cuellar notched the clinching victory in Game No. 5, with Frank again hitting a homer. Brooks, who batted .429 and was named the Most Valuable Player, was accorded a standing ovation after taking a called strike in his final at bat.

At the other end of the spectrum, Brooks proved only that he was human when he made 3 errors in one inning—2 on one play—in a game against the Oakland A's on July 28, 1971. Brooksie also grounded into 2 double plays and fouled to the catcher that memorable night. But, not to worry. Fellow Hall of Famer Frank Robinson took him off the hook with a 3-run homer in the 9th, providing a

THE TWO CHARTER
MEMBERS OF THE ORIOLES
HALL OF FAME.

★

3-2 victory.

One of Frank's finest moments in an Orioles' uniform came in the sixth game of the 1971 World Series when his daring on the bases kept the O's alive to fight another day.

The Orioles, seeking to repeat as World Champions, had won the first 2 games of the series at home rather easily. Dave McNally pitched a 3-hitter and retired 21 of the last 22 Pittsburgh batters to win the opener 5-3, with the help of Merv Rettenmund's 3-run homer and solo roundtrippers by Frank and Don Buford.

The Orioles had no homers, but 14 singles and 8 walks, in the 11-3 second game victory behind Jim Palmer—who drove in 2 runs with bases-loaded walks. Rettunmund tied a World Series record with 2 hits in one inning, as the O's scored 6 runs in the fifth.

The Pirates won all 3 games in Pittsburgh, but Frank was the catalyst who kept the Orioles alive when they returned home and won 3-2 in 10 innings. Frank singled with one out and moved to third on a single by Rettenmund, despite being hobbled with an injury to his right Achilles tendon. To make matters worse, he pulled a muscle in his left thigh while avoiding the tag.

Still, when Brooks flied to medium center, Frank was able to

WHAT ELSE WAS NEW?
BROOKSIE FOILS THE
BIG RED MACHINE ONE
MORE TIME.

★

FRANK ROBBY DESPITE SEVERELY AILING LEGS SCORED THE
WINNING RUN IN THE 10TH INNING ON BROOKS' SHORT
SACRIFICE FLY TO CENTER TO TIE THE BUCS AT 3 GAMES
APIECE IN THE 1971 WORLD SERIES.

★

BROOKSIE GETS A STANDING
OVATION AFTER TAKING A
CALLED THIRD STRIKE, HIS
LAST AT BAT IN HIS SPECTACU-
LAR '70 WORLD SERIES.

scramble home ahead of the throw from Vic Davalillo to score the winning run, forcing a 7th game. But, Frank's heroics only delayed Pittsburgh's eventual triumph. Steve Blass, who beat the Orioles on a 3-hitter in the third game, allowed just 4 hits in the finale and edged Mike Cuellar 2-1 in a stirring pitchers' duel.

When Frank hit a home run completely out of Memorial Stadium on May 8, 1966, a crowd of 49,516, including 11,858 non-paying Safety Patrol youngsters, was on hand for the historic "first."

That turnout was a far cry from that of Aug 17, 1972, when an afternoon makeup game drew a crowd (???) of 655, a rare major league attendance figure small enough to be played in Maryland's Pick 3 lottery.

About 2 months after Frank's titanic homer, Boog Powell tied an American League record at Memorial Stadium, driving in 11 runs during a July 6 doubleheader against Kansas City. He had 2 homers and 2 doubles. One homer was a grand slam, and he just missed another with a long sacrifice fly.

Frank was kind to local fans with his milestone hits. He connected for career home run No. 400 in Memorial Stadium, off Minnesota's Jim Kaat on Sep 9, 1967; recorded his 2,500th hit, a 3-run homer, against Washington's Horacio Pina on July 8, 1971, and hit home run No. 500 off Detroit's Fred Scherman on Sep 13, 1971, in the second game of a twi-night doubleheader.

Unfortunately, the crowd that night totaled only 13,292, and Frank didn't reach the 500 plateau until the ninth inning of the second game (Beware of those who said they witnessed this event).

Two of Frank's teammates reached significant milestones at Memorial Stadium in 1974. Boog Powell hit home run No. 300 (he finished with 303 as an Oriole) in the first game of a doubleheader on Sep 13 off Dick Bosman of Cleveland. Bosman later was to join the Orioles' organization as a minor league pitching coach.

Earlier that season, Brooks Robinson rapped out his 2,600th hit (his career total reached 2,842) in a June 7 game against Texas. That continued Brooks' noteworthy feats against the Washington-Texas franchise. He also had his 2,000th and 2,300th hits and his 1,000th rbi against those pesky Senators/ Rangers.

★
ARGUABLY THE MOST EXCITING AND MOST UNEXPECTED FINISH OF A BIG GAME IN ORIOLES HISTORY. WITH TWO OUT IN THE BOTTOM OF THE 12TH, IN THE FIRST ALCS GAME EVER PLAYED ('69), PAUL BLAIR, IN A TERRIBLE SLUMP, DROPPED A BUNT DOWN THE 3RD BASE LINE AND MARK BELANGER SCAMPERED HOME WITH THE WINNING RUN...RON PERRANOSKI AND JOHN ROSEBORO WERE THE TWINS BATTERY.

Less than 2 weeks later, Bobby Grich hit 3 homers off Minnesota in a June 18 game, the first Oriole to accomplish that feat at home.

Memorial Stadium also was the site, in 1974, of native Baltimorean Al Kaline's 3000th hit. With his parents watching, the Southern High School graduate became the 12th player to reach that milestone by slicing a double to right off Dave McNally in the Sep 24 game.

Local fans cheered the future Hall of Famer, but reserved their loudest outburst for the Orioles, who rallied to defeat Detroit 5-4 and took over first place to stay in the American League. Brooks doubled home the tying run in the eighth, and later scored on a squeeze bunt by Andy Etchebarren.

The Orioles won 28 of their last 34 games that season to overcome an 8-game Boston lead, and then New York, for the AL East title. The O's won their last 9, 5 at home, to win by 2 games and beat the Yanks for the first time in a stretch drive (They'd lost 2 pennant races to the Bombers in the last 2 weeks, in '60 and '64).

The Yanks, the big, bad bullies of baseball both before and after the Orioles rejoined the American League in 1954, always seemed to bring out the best in the Orioles.

Despite a 37-67 record against New York in the 8 seasons thru 1990, the Orioles still held the best lifetime record against the Yankees (308-313, .496).

During the period under discussion here, the O's were 101-56 (.643) against the Baltimore fans most-hated rival. At home, the pace was an even more productive .675 (54-26). The fans loved it.

What's more, the Orioles' records for most hits (9) and most runs (10) in an inning first came against New York on July 8, 1969. The widest margin of victory, 17-0 over Chicago, came a couple of weeks later, on July 27.

The club's longest game also came at home, the O's beating the Washington Senators 7-5 on Andy Etchebarren's two-run homer in the 19th inning, on June 4, 1967. The game began at 2:04 p.m. and

THE COLORS WERE AWFUL, BUT THIS QUARTET WAS AWESOME IN '71. FOUR 20-GAME WINNERS IN ONE SEASON: MIKE CUELLAR, PAT DOBSON, DAVE MCNALLY, JIM PALMER...THE ORIOLES WORE THOSE UNIFORMS FOR ONLY A FEW WEEKS BEFORE CONSIGNING THEM TO WELL-DESERVED OBLIVION.

ended at 7:22, much too long for a "getaway day." Immediately after the game, the Orioles departed on a trip to the West Coast.

Orioles' pitchers also have had noteworthy performances in Memorial Stadium, the site for all 4 of the club's no-hitters.

Hoyt Wilhelm pitched the first no-no in club history against the Yanks on Sep 20, 1958, but the next 3 were notched in consecutive years during "The Dynasty Era."

The first, on Apr 30, 1967, resulted in ambivalent feelings for Orioles' fans, who first cheered Steve Barber on his budding no-hitter, and then suffered when Detroit won 2-1 even without a hit. One run scored in the ninth on a wild pitch by Barber, and the other on an error before reliever Stu Miller could get the last out.

Just about a year later, on Apr 27, 1968, Baltimorean Tom Phoebus pitched a no-hitter against Boston, fanning 9, in a game which started one hour and 23 minutes late because of rain. Brooks (who else?) saved the day for Phoebus, snaring a liner by Rico Petrocelli in the eighth inning.

Jim Palmer, who had 5 one-hitters, pitched the lone no-hitter of his career (barring a comeback in the 21st Century) on Aug 13, 1969, just 4 days after coming off the disabled list. He walked 6 and struck out 8.

The end of the dynasty did not mean the end of miracles at Memorial Stadium. Many more memorable sights and sounds were to follow.

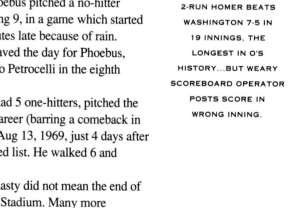

ANDY ETCHEBARREN'S 2-RUN HOMER BEATS WASHINGTON 7-5 IN 19 INNINGS, THE LONGEST IN O'S HISTORY...BUT WEARY SCOREBOARD OPERATOR POSTS SCORE IN WRONG INNING.

MANAGER EARL WEAVER AND BROADCASTER CHUCK THOMPSON ADMIRE 1970 WORLD SERIES TROPHY..

Memorable Moments BY BOT RODA

GOLD GLOVER PAUL BLAIR MAKES ANOTHER SPECTACULAR CATCH.

SKYDIVER IN BIRD COSTUME MAKES OPENING DAY LEAP. MISSED MOUND AND ENDS UP IN PARKING LOT.

ROCKY COLAVITO'S RECORD TYING 4 HOMERS HERE FOR CLEVELAND ON JUNE 10, 1959.

① WILLIE TASBY PLAYING CENTERFIELD IN HIS STOCKING FEET, '58, DURING A THUNDERSTORM... AFRAID HIS SPIKES WOULD DRAW LIGHTNING.

② FRANK ROBINSON'S HOME RUN IN '66 OFF CLEVELAND'S LUIS TIANT THAT WENT OUT OF THE PARK. (STILL THE ONLY ONE)

③ CHUCK DIERING'S CATCH OF MICKEY MANTLE'S 440' DRIVE INTO THE HEDGE. '55

④ '84 OPENER-PRESIDENT REAGAN, COMMISSIONER BOWIE KUHN, OWNER EDWARD BENNETT WILLIAMS POSE FOR WHITE HOUSE PRESS CORPS--O'S MGR ALTOBELLI FORCED TO STAND AT OTHER END OF DUGOUT TO SEE THE GAME.

⑤ "LEATHER CURTAIN -- TRIBUTE TO GREAT DEFENSIVE INFIELDERS THE O'S HAVE HAD -- 3B-ROBINSON, SS-APARICIO, BELANGER & RIPKEN 2B-JOHNSON, ADAIR, GRICH, DAUER & B. RIPKEN.

⑥ 8/23/83 RELIEVER TIPPY MARTINEZ PICKS OFF 3 BLUE JAYS AT 1ST IN ONE INNING.

⑦ BILLY O'DELL HITS 2 RUN INSIDE THE PARK HOMER-- BOUNCES ON WOODEN FOUL LINE & OVER AL SMITH'S HEAD.

⑧ LATE 70'S--WILD BILL HAGY, FOLK HERO HANGS OUT WITH DISCIPLES IN UPPER SECTION 34.

⑨ BASE SWEEPER LINDA WAREHIME SWATS 3RD BASE COACH IN FANNY WITH BROOM.

⑩ THE BIRD AND BALL GIRLS DANCE ON 3RD BASE DUGOUT.

⑪ '83 WORLD SERIES--JOHN DENVER SINGS "COUNTRY BOY" ON TOP OF DUGOUT.

⑫ MIKE DEVEREAUX' CONTROVERSIAL GAME WINNING HOMER THAT UMPS RULED SOARED PAST THE FOUL POLE IN FAIR TERRITORY. WAS THE GAME WINNER IN 9TH VS. ANGELS 7/15/89

⑬ 8' DROP FROM 1ST ROW OF BOX SEATS BEFORE FIELD BOXES INSTALLED '61.

⑭ HEDGE RUNNING FROM LEFT TO RIGHT CENTER.

COME TO BIRDLAND

HERE

SEAT MIN CA OAK TEX KC CHI

	1 2 3 4 5 6 7 8 9 10	R H E
CIN	3 0 0 0 0 0 0 0 0	3 6 0
BAL	2 2 2 0 1 0 0 2	9 15 0

WP: CUELLAR LP: MERRITT
SERIES MVP: B ROBINSON WORLD CHAMPS: THE O'S

"NEW" SCOREBOARD NOW KNOWN AS "OLD SCOREBOARD"

SPLIT POW

POOF!

OLD GOLF CART USED TO BRING IN RELIEVERS

O'S OUTFIELDER LOPEZ ATTEMPTING WHILE BALL

BOOG POWELL & EDDIE MURRAY-- 2 LEADING HR HITTERS IN O'S HISTORY

GROUNDSKEEPER PAT SANTARONE'S TOMATO PATCH IN LEFT FIELD

"LEATHER CURTAIN"

3RD BASE COACH BILLY HUNTER

PRESS

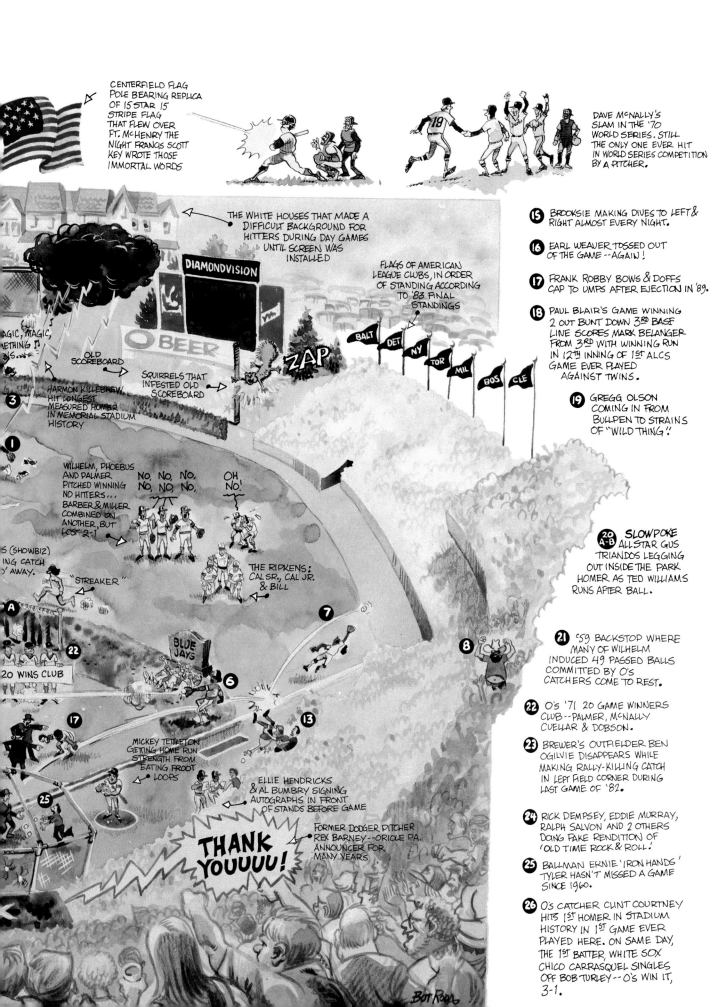

You Can Still Hear the Echo...

BY JOHN STEADMAN

*O*n Sunday afternoons in autumn and winter you can still hear the echo.

A gauntlet of musicians, attired in blue and white uniforms, the proud band of the Baltimore Colts, formed a human tunnel from the dugout to the goal line. Their team was about to be introduced. And then came the deafening roar, exploding from human throats, and reverberating around this massive arena made of concrete and mortar but filled more with heart and soul.

The love affair with the Baltimore Colts was real. Loud. Boisterous. Profound. The sound waves flowing from the seats in Memorial Stadium shocked the opposition and rattled windows in neighborhood houses. The Colts were soon to kick off. The noise never abated more than a decibel or two. A sports writer from the Chicago Tribune, one Cooper Rollow, looked upon the scene from the press box and quickly confirmed it as "the world's largest outdoor insane asylum."

Oh, the memories. There was a commensurate amount of fun in the stands as there was finesse and force on the field. That correlation is in no way exaggerated. First there was Willie (The Rooter) Andrews, who marched about the premises under a horse's head of papier mache. He once skipped a car payment so he would have enough money to accompany the team on a fan-tour road trip.

And, along came Hurst (Loudy) Loudenslager, who wasn't loud at all but became the most loyal

fan any team ever had. He created a museum for the Colts in his home and went to the airport to offer hopeful farewells to the players as they departed and greetings when they returned from road trips. He met them, literally, coming and going, regardless of the hour. He'd station himself at the gate to the plane while a rendition of the Colts' fight song emanated from a record player or tape cassette.

The spectators, not all Willie The Rooters or Loudy Loudenslagers, were nonetheless integral parts of the proceedings. The Colts were a team that accommodated Baltimore so comfortably. Even the name, Colts, suggested Baltimore's romantic past with the horse...riding them, racing them, and betting on them at Pimlico. And, besides, Colts fit perfectly in any newspaper headline.

The Colts' name was born of public interest, evolving from a contest in 1947, the first year the team was in business. The winning suggestion was by Charles Evans of Middle River, MD. And then came an appropriately named player, the aptly dubbed Lamar (Racehorse) Davis, a swift-striking, go-deep pass receiver, safetyman and kick returner. "Racehorse" Davis was meant to be a Colt. Much later came Alan (The Horse) Ameche, who went untouched for a 79-yard touchdown stroll the first

★

EXCITEMENT AND DRAMA UNFOLD WHEN THE COLTS ARE INTRODUCED. DON SHULA (NO.25), ROYCE WOMBLE (NO.26), BILLY VESSELS (NO. 27) AND ALAN "THE HORSE" AMECHE (NO.35) LEAD THE WAY FROM TUNNEL TO THE MEMORIAL STADIUM FIELD. IT'S KICKOFF TIME.

JIM PARKER, GUARD-TACKLE, IS ONLY COLT IN BOTH PRO AND COLLEGE FOOTBALL HALLS OF FAME.

LENNY MOORE, WHO IS CONSIDERED THE MOST EXPLOSIVE RUNNER-RECEIVER IN HISTORY OF NFL.

GINO MARCHETTI HAD A WAY OF INTIMIDATING QUARTERBACKS. HE WAS A ONE MAN "SACK PACK," STRONG AND QUICK OFF THE SCRIMMAGE LINE.

RAYMOND BERRY RETIRED IN 1967 AS THE THEN LEADING PASS RECEIVER IN ANNALS OF THE GAME.

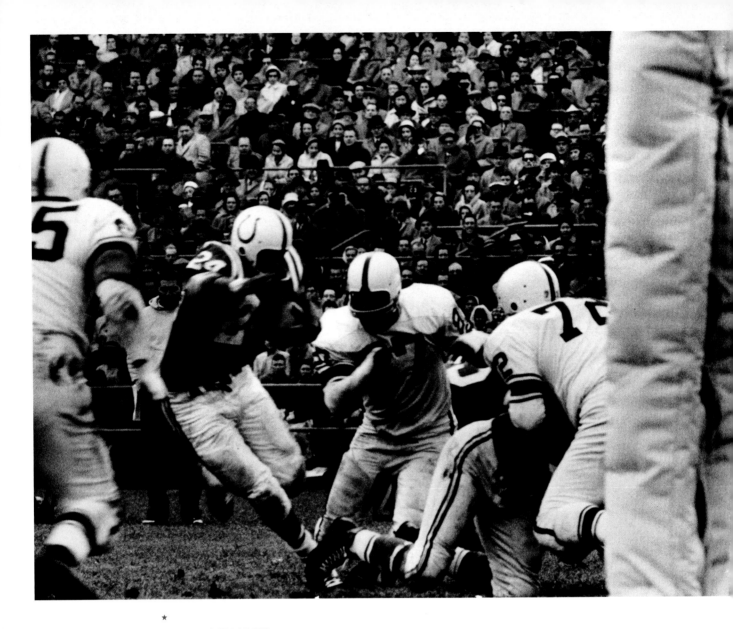

★

LENNY MOORE DISPLAYS AMAZING GRACE AND
BALANCE AS HE ACCELERATES TOWARDS THE GOAL
LINE. HE TRANSMITTED EXPLOSIVE EXCITEMENT.

time he ever touched the ball in a professional
game. If there was a disappointment in linguistic
linkage it would be that the Colts drafted but never
signed a halfback from Louisiana State University
who was known as LeRoy (The Black Stallion)
Labat.

In 35 years of professional football, first in the
All-America Conference for three seasons and then
the NFL, the Colts had nine Hall of Fame players
and one coach. Their names, in order of selection,
are Art Donovan, Joe Perry, Y. A. Tittle, Gino
Marchetti, Raymond Berry, Jim Parker, Lenny
Moore, John Unitas, Ted Hendricks, and Coach
Weeb Ewbank. Their accomplishments created a
legacy and helped establish tradition that will never
die—even if the team was unceremoniously stuffed
into moving vans and carted away under the cover
of darkness on a miserable March night in 1984.

AFTER COLTS WHIPPED NEW YORK GIANTS FOR 1958 CROWN AT YANKEE
STADIUM, MAYOR THOMAS D'ALESANDRO, JR., VISITED WITH JOHN UNITAS
AND ALAN "THE HORSE" AMECHE. IT WAS BALTIMORE'S MOST MEMORABLE
FOOTBALL GAME IN HISTORY, PLUS HELPING TO LIFT THE NFL TO NEW
HEIGHTS OF ACCEPTANCE.

★

Frequent sellouts were reported but nothing like the 51 straight the Colts tried to convey. Still, getting a ticket, at any time, was a difficult assignment. From 1957 through 1971, the "Unitas Years," they were never under .500. In 1958 and 1959, they won the world championship in confrontations against the New York Giants, and then remained perennial challengers. In 1964, the Colts won the Western Division but lost the title to the Cleveland Browns. Their first Super Bowl, after the 1968 season, was a disastrous loss to the New York Jets after being installed a 16 1/2- point favorite. Two years later, they defeated the Dallas Cowboys for the Super Bowl prize. But their most historic attainment came with the defeat of the Giants in 1958, at Yankee Stadium, when destiny permitted the Colts to be the first team in football history to win in sudden-death overtime, 23-17.

The next year they were the home team for the championship and again put away the Giants. It was the only title ever decided in Baltimore, 31-16, Dec. 27, before 57,545 onlookers on a surprisingly warm afternoon at Memorial Stadium. Pat Summerall kicked three field goals for the Giants, and they led, 9-7, entering the fourth period. The Colts' John Sample and Andy Nelson made interceptions and that broke it open. Unitas

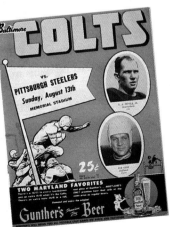

A LOOK BACK AT A 1950 COLTS-STEELERS GAME PROGRAM.

★

passed for touchdowns to Moore and Jerry Richardson, ran in one himself and watched as Sample returned an interception for a score and Steve Myhra connected on a field goal.

If there is one game, though, that set itself apart from all the others it would be the 1958 conquest of the San Francisco 49ers. The 49ers were leading, 27-7, at halftime but the Colts, triggered by a third period dash of 74 yards by Lenny Moore, rocketed ahead to win by 35-27. It meant the Western Division title for the Colts and three weeks later they beat the Giants in overtime—what is euphemistically referred to as "the greatest game ever played." But most of the players, even to this day, vote the win over the 49ers as their most auspicious and satisfying result of all time. It qualifies as the greatest comeback in the 35 years the club was in Baltimore. Two neutral observers, announcers Chuck Thompson and Vince Bagli, agree.

At that point in time, the city was "Coltafide." Parents were moved to name their children after the heroes they cheered on Sunday afternoons, which is why there are young men, now adults in Baltimore, with names of Gino, Lenny, Raymond, Alan, John, and even a Colt Taylor.

Organizers of oyster roasts and even some weddings scheduled around the Colts' games. They knew if there was a conflict, their attendance

Suddenly, he decided to divorce himself from the ball and threw it up in the air, where the Colts' Jim Castiglia retrieved it and stepped into the end zone. Touchdown Baltimore.

That first edition of the Colts, put in operation by a Washington-based ownership group headed by Bob Rodenberg and Herb Bryant, which also included Maury Nee, Karl Corby and Baltimoreans Charles P. McCormick, R.C. (Jake) Embry and Al Wheltle, were the pioneers. Wilson (Bud) Schwenk, Billy Hillenbrand, Augie Lio and Hub Bechtol, along with "Racehorse" Davis, became the early player favorites. The Colts' band paraded, the team wore green and silver uniforms and Baltimore was off and running to the football races. Success, despair, jubilation and, in

would be minimal. The way Baltimore embraced the Colts was more than merely giving a good substantial yell for the old home team. It became so warm and personal.

The victories by the Colts in Memorial Stadium coined such newspaper banner lines as "Miracle on 33rd Street," the "House of Thrills," and a special corner of the end zone known as "Orrsville," since that was where Jimmy Orr caught so many touchdown passes after making slick moves to get open. The names and personalities of the players had gained wide prominence, be it a Bill Pellington, Jim Mutscheller, Dick Szymanski, Gene (Big Daddy) Lipscomb, Ordell Braase, Joe Campanella, Elmer Wingate, Sisto Averno, Madison (Buzz) Nutter, and Don Shula, first as a player, then a coach.

We were there when it all started, Sep. 7, 1947, against the Brooklyn Dodgers of the All-America Conference and then, finally, for the last time, Dec. 18, 1983, versus the Houston Oilers. A beginning and an end. Much of what happened in between was charged with excitement and offered an ongoing appreciation for the purity of physical and mental execution, such as Unitas connecting with Berry on a sideline pass or firing to Moore deep along the sidelines or Marchetti and Donovan pressuring a rival quarterback or "Big Daddy" chasing down a ball carrier.

The Colts inaugural game in 1947, played on a humid, rainy afternoon, qualifies as the most bizarre opening any team ever had...The cue occurring on the opening kickoff. The ball was fielded by a Brooklyn Dodger halfback named Elmore Harris, who had played at Morgan State, and returned to near midfield. Tackled hard, he lost possession but it was picked up by a teammate, guard Harry Buffington. Amazingly, Buffington began to run towards the goal line. Only it was the wrong one.

the end, when the team was pulled away, abandonment.

In 1948, their second season, the Colts became more than respectable. They tied for the Eastern Division and, in a playoff with the Buffalo Bills, for the right to meet the Cleveland Browns for the championship, came within a disputed call by an official of doing just that. The Colts were ahead in the game in the second half when the Bills' George Ratterman passed to Chet Mutryn, who made a clean catch and continued to run. Tackled by Dick Barwegen, he fumbled and the Colts' John Mellus recovered. But Tommy Whelan, the head linesman, signaled an incomplete pass and Buffalo, not Baltimore, had the ball. The Bills went in to score, got another

OFF-BALANCE CATCHES BECAME ROUTINE FOR RAYMOND BERRY. DEVOTION TO DUTY, MEANING PRACTICE, PRACTICE AND MORE PRACTICE, ALLOWED HIM TO BECOME AN EXTRAORDINARY PASS RECEIVER. LEAVING THE STADIUM, USUALLY CARRYING A BOOK AND WEARING GLASSES, OFTEN FOUND HIM GOING UNRECOGNIZED BY SPECTATORS WHO ONLY MOMENTS BEFORE HAD CHEERED CATCHES SUCH AS THIS ONE.

★

BERT RECHICHAR, ONE OF THE FIRST COLT HEROES, KICKS WHILE TOM KEANE HOLDS IN THIS 1953 ACTION.

★

"GLADIATOR"

ONE OF THE TRUE
CLASSIC PICTURES
OF ART DONOVAN,
PROJECTING SIDELINE
INTENSITY, WAS MADE
BY PHOTOGRAPHER
MORTON TADDER.
IT'S A GRAPHIC STUDY
OF A FOOTBALL
WARRIOR. DONOVAN,
STRONG AND SMART,
WAS THE FIRST COLT
ELECTED TO PRO
FOOTBALL HALL OF
FAME.

touchdown and moved ahead to win, 28-17. A near riot ensued at the end when thousands of fans invaded the field to threaten Whelan. It was a bad scene, one of the worst in the city's long sports history. Buffalo players, recognizing that Whelan was in serious trouble, came to rescue him from the crowd. They let him enter their locker room and, for precaution, took him away from the stadium on their chartered team bus.

The Colts had high hopes for 1949, but they never materialized, and in 1950 hit a low point when they won only one game in their first NFL season. The hero of that only victorious day, Jim Spavital, a fullback from Oklahoma A&M, was carried off the field by the elated spectators. Baltimore was being acclaimed for its football enthusiasm, so much so that Tarzan Taylor, a line coach under the first head coach, Cecil Isbell, called Baltimore "a big Green Bay." It was a compliment that said much for Baltimore since Green Bay came close to making the Packers a religion.

In 1951 and 1952, the Colts were on the sidelines, the franchise being forfeited by a pseudo owner, Abe (Shorty) Watner, for $50,000 to the league. Its players, including Y.A. Tittle, Art Donovan, Art Spinney, Billy Stone, Herb Rich, Ed King, later to become governor of Massachusetts,

and all others were put into the common player draft for redistribution. But Baltimore wasn't about to let the NFL get away with that illegal act, and the league, to avoid a serious lawsuit, agreed to place another club in Baltimore, which is how the Dallas Texans, which were bankrupt at the time, became the Colts of 1953.

By then, Baltimore was constructing a new stadium, on the same location that had been utilized since 1922. The old wooden structure, which had housed the Colts' earlier version and the International League Orioles, was being replaced with the first stage of a concrete double-tier facility, paid for by the City. As they opened the 1953 campaign, the capacity was only 23,715. However, because of the on-going construction, in hopes of attracting a big league baseball club, it increased each week as the contractor progressed with work and added more seats. The Colts return to the NFL was momentous in that they

PRESS GUIDES FROM
THE BALTIMORE COLTS'
EVENTFUL PAST.

★

ENDOWED WITH A SMOOTH
DELIVERY AND OUTSTANDING
RANGE QUALIFIED Y.A. TITTLE AS
ONE OF THE MOST STYLISH
THROWERS OF A FOOTBALL AT ANY
LEVEL OF COMPETITION. SOME
ADMIRERS SAID HIS INITIALS, Y.A.,
STOOD FOR "YARD ARM." ACTU-
ALLY, HIS GIVEN NAME WAS
YELBERTON ABRAHAM. THE FIRST
THREE YEARS OF A CAREER THAT
CARRIED HIM TO THE HALL OF
FAME WERE SPENT AS A COLTS'
QUARTERBACK.

★

upset the Chicago Bears and Bert Rechichar, a safetyman who had been blind in one eye since birth, kicked a record 56-yard field goal. It was something he had never tried in college or pro yet the ball carried far and true. It was such an astounding achievement that Robert Ripley later carried it in his syndicated newspaper feature, "Believe It Or Not."

The owner of the restored franchise was Carroll Rosenbloom, who had been recruited by Commissioner Bert Bell. Men in the business community such as Tom Mullan, Sr., Zanvyl Krieger, Bill Hilgenberg, R.C. (Jake) Embry and Bruce Livie, who had led the civic campaign to sell 15,000 season tickets before Rosenbloom arrived, championed the drive, and supplied the financial stability. Keith Molesworth was named coach and Don Kellett the general manager, the appointments virtually handpicked by Commissioner Bell. Oddly enough, both had been standout minor league baseball players and, for a brief time, had been the double-play combination for the Syracuse Chiefs of the International League.

After a 3-9 season, with Claude (Buddy) Young the standout player, Rosenbloom and Kellett moved Molesworth into a scouting position, evaluating talent, and hired Wilbur (Weeb) Ewbank, an assistant coach of the Cleveland Browns. Ewbank promised results in what he called a "five-year plan," and it took exactly that long to hit the jackpot. It was their extreme good fortune to receive a postcard from an unknown correspondent in Pittsburgh who was touting the prowess of a young quarterback playing for the semi-pro Bloomfield Rams, one John Constantine Unitas. The Colts had remembered Unitas from the previous college draft, when he had been picked by his hometown Pittsburgh Steelers, and followed up with a long-distance phone call that

MORE OFTEN THAN NOT BILL PELLINGTON (NO. 36) AND GINO MARCHETTI (NO. 89) WERE AROUND THE BALL CARRIER. HERE THEY PREPARE TO SANDWICH FRANK GIFFORD (NO. 16) IN THIS COLTS-GIANTS COLLISION. MARCHETTI, DEFENSIVE END, AND PELLINGTON, AN OUTSIDE LINEBACKER, WERE WITH THE COLTS FROM 1953 THROUGH 1964. THEIR FIRST TEAM FINISHED IN LAST PLACE BUT, FIVE YEARS LATER, THEY CLIMBED TO THE WORLD CHAMPIONSHIP.

★

cost them 85 cents. This was their only investment in signing the player who became the game's most consummate quarterback. His first contract was for a salary of $7,000 (no bonus), but he had to stay with the team the entire year to be paid.

Unitas was the catalyst. He had such other standouts around him as Ameche, Donovan, Marchetti, Braase, Mutscheller, Parker, Spinney, Moore, Don Joyce, Don Shinnick, Bill Pellington, L.G. (Long Gone) Dupre, George Preas, Alex Sandusky, and others of superb style and talent. They quickly became the most talked-about team in the NFL. They were to win the celebrated 1958 championship against the New York Giants. And the next year, repeated against the Giants, only this time in Baltimore.

The Colts were difficult to defense. Unitas was either pitching to Berry, Mutscheller, or Moore, or handing off to Ameche, Moore, or Dupre. Ameche had sure hands, too, and handled flare passes flawlessly and rarely, if ever, fumbled. Moore was a flamboyant show stopper. That 74-yard zig-zag run against the 49ers in the Western Division win of 1958 was laced with speed, clever moves, changing pace, leaning one way and recovering to go another and, in the end, an unbelievable result. Frank Gifford, a rival halfback, who later joined Moore in the Hall of Fame, says he is the best combination receiver/runner he has ever seen. Case closed.

With euphoria exploding all-around, tickets to the Colts were difficult to buy. Attending Colts games was the "in" thing to do, and they were running out of room in a stadium that held 60,586 for football. The band marched and, the cheerleaders, founded in 1954 by Thelma Mack, its first organizer and captain (six years before the Dallas Cowboys), gave Baltimore a character all its own. The helmets took on a distinctive

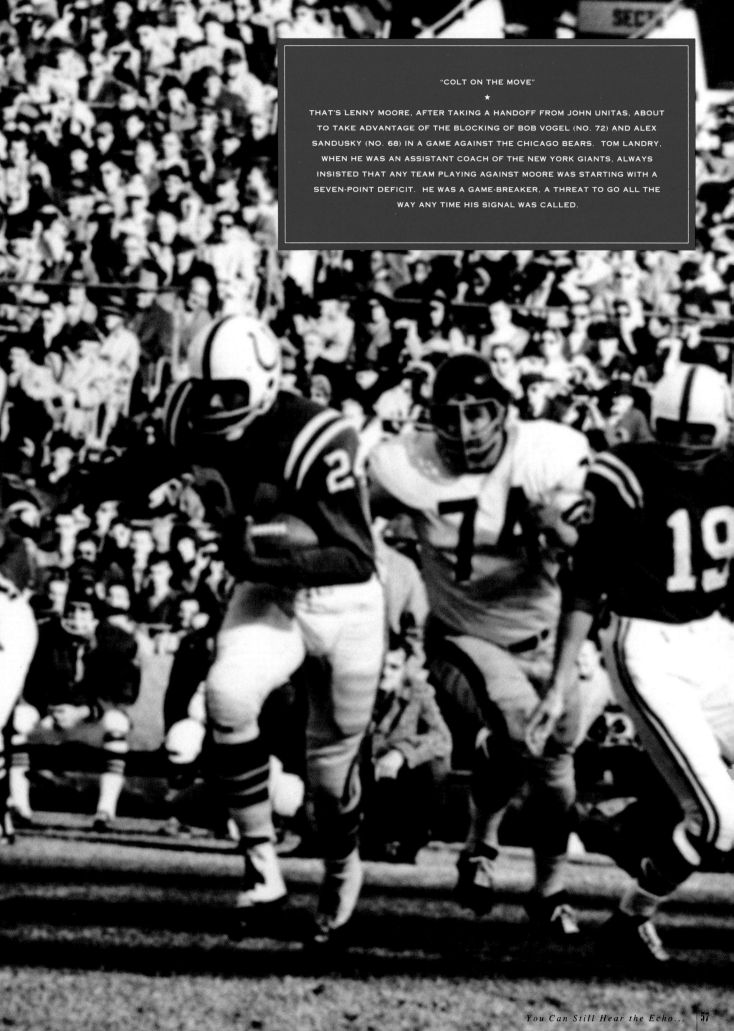

"COLT ON THE MOVE"

★

THAT'S LENNY MOORE, AFTER TAKING A HANDOFF FROM JOHN UNITAS, ABOUT
TO TAKE ADVANTAGE OF THE BLOCKING OF BOB VOGEL (NO. 72) AND ALEX
SANDUSKY (NO. 68) IN A GAME AGAINST THE CHICAGO BEARS. TOM LANDRY,
WHEN HE WAS AN ASSISTANT COACH OF THE NEW YORK GIANTS, ALWAYS
INSISTED THAT ANY TEAM PLAYING AGAINST MOORE WAS STARTING WITH A
SEVEN-POINT DEFICIT. HE WAS A GAME-BREAKER, A THREAT TO GO ALL THE
WAY ANY TIME HIS SIGNAL WAS CALLED.

COLTS' CHEERLEADERS, ACCOMPANIED BY "DIXIE"
THE TEAM MASCOT AND RIDER, PREPARE FOR THE
KICKOFF AT MEMORIAL STADIUM.

★

★

TED MARCHIBRODA
COACHED COLTS TO THREE
CONSECUTIVE DIVISION
TITLES.

★

DON MCCAFFERTY LED WAY
TO CITY'S LONE SUPER
BOWL CHAMPIONSHIP.

★

CECIL ISBELL, COLTS
FIRST COACH.

look when Sam Banks, the team's publicity director in 1953-1954, suggested a logo be added. The Los Angeles Rams had pioneered the idea with rams' horns, the Philadelphia Eagles had wings, and now the Colts put horseshoe designs on their headgear.

The Stadium not only was the stage for Sunday afternoon games, but the team practiced there, too. With so much wear and tear given the turf, come late November and December, the field was bald. All dirt, little grass. The situation didn't change until 1980 when owner Bob Irsay built an excellent complex for the offices and training facilities in

"BLACKBOARD DRILL"

★

COACH WEEB EWBANK, EVER THE TEACHER, EXPLAINS A PLAY (LEFT TO RIGHT) TO RAYMOND
BERRY, L.G. "LONG GONE" DUPRE, ROYCE WOMBLE AND JIM "BUCKY" MUTSCHELLER.

BERT JONES, GIFTED WITH POWERFUL ARM AND RUNNING ABILITY, PREPARES TO THROW AS DON MCCAULEY (NO. 23) PUTS HIMSELF IN POSITION TO BLOCK FOR HIS QUARTERBACK.

Owings Mills. Games in Baltimore, most of the time, featured a pony mascot, wearing blue and white tack, sprinting the perimeter of the stadium after touchdowns and field goals—scored by the Colts, of course. A contest had been held to find a name and "Dixie" was chosen. Once after the Colts had put up large numbers against the Rams, a weary linebacker, Les Richter, checked the scoreboard and said, "That horse ran around the field so often I thought I was at Santa Anita." Later, escalating insurance rates, covering public appearances, priced "Dixie" out of the market. She and a series of successors were locked in the barn.

But the mascot, the band, flag line, majorettes, cheerleaders, and the official alma mater song, "Fight On, You Baltimore Colts," made Memorial Stadium a glorious place to spend a Sunday afternoon. There were three distinct phases, or eras, in the city's football story—all individually orchestrated by the then quarterback-in-charge. First it was Y.A. Tittle, next John Unitas and, finally, Bert Jones. The same with the coaches, including the likes of Cecil Isbell, the former Packer great;

END OF A NOT-SO-PERFECT DAY. THE COLTS HAD BEEN ROUTED BY THE PITTSBURGH STEELERS IN A 1976 PLAYOFF AND THEN AN AIRPLANE CRASHED IN THE SECOND DECK OF THE STADIUM. THERE WERE NO INJURIES TO SPECTATORS BECAUSE THE CROWD HAD LEFT EARLY, SOME IN THE THIRD PERIOD, AS THE STEELERS ROMPED. PILOT DONALD KRONER WAS ARRESTED FOR DISREGARDING SAFETY REGULATIONS.

★

Weeb Ewbank, Don Shula, Don McCafferty, and Ted Marchibroda. There were other coaches, too, coming and going with frequency during the Irsay regime. Those mentioned attained a measure of success, starting with Isbell who tied for a divisional title in 1948. Ewbank won back-to-back crowns in the NFL. Shula took the Colts to Super Bowl III, losing in a mighty upset to the New York Jets but, two years later, after Shula had gone to the Miami Dolphins, McCafferty gave Baltimore its only Super Bowl Trophy when his team beat the Cowboys in Super Bowl V.

There's reason and substantial evidence to minimize the Colt years under Irsay and General Manager Joe Thomas, who arbitrarily decided the team needed to be rebuilt. Unitas, Tom Matte, John Mackey, and others were ticketed elsewhere. Changes were needed, but it appeared that Thomas was more interested in remaking the franchise in his own image. However, in a comparatively short time, the Colts were winning again with young players the likes of Bert Jones, Don McCauley, Lydell Mitchell, Glenn Doughty, Roger Carr,

OFF AND RUNNING FOR A TOUCHDOWN GOES JIM MUTSCHELLER, WHO OUT DISTANCES THE CHICAGO BEARS' STAN WALLACE (NO. 40) ON HIS WAY TO THE GOAL LINE IN 1957. MUTSCHELLER WAS AN EXCEPTIONAL PASS RECEIVER WHOSE BLOCKING ABILITY CONFUSED DEFENDERS. THEY DIDN'T KNOW IF HIS INTENTIONS WERE TO BLOCK OR CATCH WHEN HE MOVED INTO THE SECONDARY, WHICH ADDED TO HIS EFFECTIVENESS.

★

PRESSURE IS EXERTED BY BUBBA SMITH (NO. 78) ON JOHN BRODIE OF THE SAN FRANCISCO 49ERS. BRODIE SAID HE COULD IDENTIFY WITH HOW IT FELT TO CRASH IN BALTIMORE, RECALLING HOW HE HAD SO MANY DIFFICULT DAYS AGAINST THE COLTS.

Raymond Chester, Bruce Laird, John Dutton, Joe Ehrmann, Fred Cook, Marty Domres, and Mike Barnes.

In 1974, a year when Howard Schnellenberger was fired as head coach and Thomas took over, the record was a dismal 2 and 12. But the next season it jumped to 10 and 4 under coach Ted Marchibroda. That represented the most imposing turnaround in NFL history. The Colts were in first place and meeting the Steelers in the playoffs in Pittsburgh. They lost 28-10, but fortunes had changed dramatically and the Colts were obviously immensely improved. They were to win the Eastern Division for the next two years but lost in the playoffs—in Baltimore to the Steelers, 40-14, in 1976 and, in double overtime to the Oakland Raiders in 1977 by a count of 37-31, on a Christmas Eve afternoon in a game that was truly a classic. The lead changed hands nine times before Ken Stabler passed to Dave Casper for the final, winning strike.

After two straight 5 and 11 showings, Marchibroda was fired, replaced by Mike McCormack and then Frank Kush. Turmoil continued.

It was just after the 1976 playoff loss to the Steelers in Baltimore's Memorial Stadium that an airplane wound up in the end zone of the second deck. A private pilot, one Donald Kroner, came in for what appeared to be a 50-yard line landing, or touchdown, but suddenly accelerated and, while endeavoring to gain altitude, fell into the top deck, as motionless as a dead bird.

Fortunately, the game had been a rout, and spectators began leaving early in the fourth quarter. Had the score been close, the crowd would have remained and there is no way to approximate the extent of casualties. It could have been a major tragedy. The pilot, who had a blue and white plane, official team colors, was hospitalized with serious but not life-threatening injuries. Ultimately, he was sentenced to a jail term after police fully documented his bizarre, life-threatening actions on the day when he literally flew into the stadium. Approaching from the north, he guided the plane between the scoreboard and an outfield light tower. A frightening scene.

The picture of the airplane wedged in the upper deck was page one in newspapers around the country and even in various parts of the world. John Brodie, a San Francisco 49ers' quarterback, who never made the mistake of taking himself too seriously, had more bad afternoons in Baltimore than he wanted to remember. "When I saw that picture of the plane," he quipped, "I knew I wasn't the only one who crashed in Memorial Stadium."

All through Unitas' golden career, the team was a consistent contender, proving his value as a leader and an athlete. He was mentally and physically strong, beyond intimidation, composed under fire, astute at recognizing defenses and could pass long or short with equal facility. In his last game for the Colts, Dec. 3, 1972, before his contract was sold to the San Diego Chargers, he left in appropriate style. The ball was lofted high in the air, almost a sky-rocket, so different than his line drive spirals, and it was coming down in a cluster of Buffalo Bills, all would-be interceptors. Almost miraculously, Eddie Hinton got his hands on it, escaped the surrounding traffic and ran for a touchdown. It was Unitas' sign-off, the last time he put his signature on a touchdown pass for the Colts. Earlier, an airplane, on a different mission from the one that crashed, had

JOHN UNITAS ENJOYED A SPECIAL MOMENT WHEN HE MADE HIS PUBLIC FAREWELL TO THE FANS WHO HAD WATCHED HIM DURING HIS 17 YEARS WITH THE COLTS. HIS ACCEPTANCE INTO THE HALL OF FAME DREW "YES" VOTES FROM EVERY SELECTOR. THAT'S JOHN'S MOTHER ON FAR LEFT, MOTHER-IN-LAW, WIFE SANDY AND SON JOEY LOOKING ON AT CEREMONY.

★

flown high above the stadium trailing a banner that read: "Unitas We Stand." It had been arranged by a group of friends, including former teammate, Ordell Braase, who was in the stadium rooting for John just like everybody else.

By that time, owner Rosenbloom had left Baltimore for the sun and glamour of Los Angeles, where he bought the Rams from the estate of the late Dan Reeves. It was a convoluted deal with Irsay, a Skokie (IL) air conditioning contractor, who first bought the Rams for a figure reported variously at between $16 million and $19 million and then trading, team-for-team, to get the Colts.

Rosenbloom avoided paying an immense sum in capital gains and, as part of the transaction, left $2 million in the Colts' coffers. The arrangement was approved by the NFL and passed scrutiny of the Internal Revenue Service.

The Stadium, on game days, dealt in excitement. There was more than football. The color imparted by the band, the cheerleaders, the "Colt Corral" fan clubs offered an appropriate backdrop. Some of the unusual things that transpired were extraordinary, such as a rival player setting up the first touchdown in their opening game by running the wrong way; Bert Rechichar establishing a field goal record the first time he ever kicked; and Alan (The Horse) Ameche galloping for a touchdown, 79 yards, untouched, on his first play as a pro. Then, don't forget, Mike Curtis tackling a fan from Rochester, NY, who invaded the field and tried to pilfer the game ball in broad daylight. That, and a lot more.

If there was an emotional moment transcending all others it was the retirement of Art Donovan on Sep. 16, 1962. He didn't want to put on a uniform

Will Rogers Never met Irsay.

IT HAD NO RIGHT TO END THIS WAY BUT IT DID. THE COLTS WERE PACKED OUT OF BALTIMORE IN MOVING VANS FOR INDIANAPOLIS ON MARCH 28, 1984. THE ACT OF PLUNDER BROUGHT ABOUT THE DEMISE OF FOOTBALL IN A CITY THAT HAD A FRANCHISE FOR 35 UNFORGETTABLE YEARS.

★

that day, saying he merely wanted to walk out for the ceremony in casual street clothes. Lou Grasmick, a business and community leader, planned the program and insisted Art had to wear full uniform. Donovan reluctantly agreed but then didn't want to put on the cumbersome shoulder pads. Again, Grasmick prevailed, asking that he appear on the field for the last time as he had looked when he was getting ready to play. Donovan made it to the 50-yard line, with 54,796 admiring spectators looking on in awe.

A committee headed by Bob Robertson, numbering 35 members, had raised contributions to buy Art a Cadillac and other gifts. After graciously accepting the presents and listening to the tributes, Donovan talked about Baltimore and what it meant to him. "Up in Heaven," he said, as a climax, "there is a lady who is happy the City of Baltimore was so good to her son—a kid from the Bronx." With that he turned and made his exit, fading off, first under the goal post and then disappearing into the dugout and finally the tunnel to the dressing room. He was crying so hard his giant body trembled all over. And, in the Stadium, those watching and listening to his farewell, were equally moved and choked with emotion.

Yes, Memorial Stadium has its memories...where a football team provided so much pleasure for 35 years and had a fanatical legion of followers, cheering legends of the game. This was the place to be, the noise resembling a volcano erupting as the packed stands boomed the lettered cheer of C-O-L-T-S.

On Sunday afternoons in autumn and winter you can still hear the echo.

OLD ORIOLE PARK BURNS ON THE NIGHT AND MORNING OF JULY 3/4, 1944, FORCING
THE INTERNATIONAL LEAGUE ORIOLES TO MOVE TO 33RD STREET.

★

It was the top of the 10th, the Orioles, leading the International League by 1 1/2 games on that July 3, 1944, were hosting the Syracuse Chiefs, and the score was tied 4-4 before an Oriole Park crowd of 6,500 fans.

Orioles manager Tommy Thomas elected to stay with his starter Ambrose "Bobo" Palica. Two walks, an error and four hits later the Chiefs led by seven, four of them crossing on a grand slam by 17-year-old shortstop Bob "Kid" Carson off the

Orioles' Jack "Rube" Keckley, also 17, who had just relieved Palica.

The Orioles went quietly in the bottom of that inning, which, as it turned out, was to be the last one ever played at Oriole Park. Before dawn of July 4, the old ballpark would be reduced to a charred shell.

As was his custom after each game, groundskeeper Mike Schofield had walked through the empty grandstand with a hose extinguishing

Out OF THE Ashes

BY FRANK LYNCH

GROUNDSKEEPER MIKE SCHOFIELD.

★

small blazes ignited by discarded cigarettes.

Twice Schofield smelled smoke and flooded those sections with water. It was close to 2 a.m. when he went to his room in the offices to rest. At about 4:20, he was awakened by the arrival of fire engines.

"It started in Section One on the third-base side," he was quoted in the Baltimore Sun. "I was able to move the batting cage out of the runway between the grandstand and pavilion in order to allow fire engines to come on the field.

"I had hardly done this when the fire swept around the park like a sheet. I never saw anything spread so fast."

While the fire was still raging, Mayor Theodore R. McKeldin appeared on the scene and officially offered the use of Municipal Stadium on 33rd Street to Orioles management. Actually, Club President George W. Reed several years earlier had already discussed such a contingency with the Park

Board and a tentative agreement had been reached.

Offers of assistance came in quickly. The Baltimore Elite Giants, members of the Negro National League, offered the use of their facility at Bugle Field on Edison Highway and Federal Street. Glenn L. Martin did the same with his newly constructed ballpark at his aircraft manufacturing plant in Middle River. The Orioles politely declined the offers and cancelled the scheduled July 4 doubleheader as well as the remainder of the brief homestand.

While the Chiefs headed for New York to acquire new uniforms and equipment, the Orioles were getting help from various sources including the Washington Senators of the American League.

One hundred and fifty uniforms, dozens of gloves, several trunkfuls of bats, balls and shoes went up in the flames. The club had just received a new consignment of 40 dozen baseballs.

Included in the loss of the park and equipment were the highly prized trophies won by the late Jack Dunn with his Orioles and prize field-trial dogs. All that remained were 25 road uniforms which trainer Eddie Weidner had sent out to be cleaned. The estimated value of the wooden park and the equipment was in excess of $150,000.

The park had been built in 1914 by the Baltimore Terrapins of the short-lived Federal League. Two years later when that league folded, Dunn moved his team into the facility, renamed it Oriole Park, and used it as a home ground for 28 1/2 years.

Newspapers of the day were filled with pictures and stories of the disaster. The most prophetic words were written by Roger H. Pippen, sports editor of the Baltimore News-Post and Sunday American.

Pippen wrote: "At the moment, what appears to be a baseball tragedy, may turn out to be a blessing in disguise. Baltimore rose from the ashes of its great fire in 1904 to be a bigger and better city. Our Orioles will come through just as soon as war

★

CONVERSION COMPLETED, THE O'S RETURNED FROM A HASTILY
SCHEDULED ROAD TRIP TO THEIR NEW HOME ON 33RD STREET. NOTE
THAT HOME PLATE WAS THEN IN WHAT IS NOW LEFT FIELD.

CLUB OWNER JACK DUNN
III, A FIGHTER PILOT IN
WORLD WAR II, AND HIS
MOTHER EXAMINE THE
RUINS. JACK WAS HOME
ON EMERGENCY LEAVE.

★

conditions permit, with a bigger and better place for its (sic) games.

"The new park will be built so that, in case the opportunity should arise, this city will return to the big leagues. The park which is today in ruins was not suitable for big league competition. You can't finance a major outfit with a seating capacity of eleven thousand."

While Municipal Stadium was being prepared for baseball, the International League rearranged the schedule to allow the Orioles to play on the road. Games were slated in Newark, Jersey City and Syracuse.

When the road trip began, the Orioles were in first place with a 39-30 record, but when they limped home for their Municipal Stadium debut on July 16, after going 3-8 on the hastily arranged trip, they were fourth at 42-38.

Those who came for the double-header against Jersey City that first day sizzled under the sun, but it was worth it. The Orioles swept the Giants, 9-3 and 10-1, and hit five homers in the process. The distinction of hitting the first home run in Municipal Stadium went to rookie catcher Sherm Lollar.

The majority of the sun-baked 12,999 fans approved of the baseball layout as constructed under the direction of Orioles Business Manager

Herb Armstrong, and so did righthanded hitters all over the International League. Many agreed the temporary, emergency job had been well done and that the new field offered an excellent test of baseball skills, except for the short leftfield (290 feet).

They liked the wide-open spaces in center and right fields which gave speedsters an opportunity to show off their talent when they drove the ball between the outfielders. There were six triples in the first two games, a sight seldom seen at Oriole Park.

Some of the negatives about the uncovered facility voiced by the fans were: beer was not sold in the stadium, a raincoat or umbrella was absolutely essential for foul weather, and fans had to sit in the sun during day games. Fortunately, there were only four more afternoon double-headers remaining on the schedule.

The double-header sweep of the Jersey City Giants was just the start of what would be a magnificent and historic homestand.

Two nights later, the Orioles' soft-spoken Kansas-born righthander named Stan West used his slider to perfection while no-hitting Jersey City, 5-0, with 9,000 fans on hand. He faced only 29 Little Giants while pitching the Orioles to within one game of the league-leading Montreal Royals. It was the first no-hitter by a Baltimore pitcher since 1907.

The next day the Orioles trailed the Newark Bears, 1-0, in the 12th with two outs and none on. Then Blas Monaco tripled off Mel Queen, and "Howitzer" Howie Moss, after working the count full, thrilled 7,500 locals by driving a Queen fastball deep into the leftfield bleachers to give Baltimore one of its most dramatic victories ever. Red Embree, who struck out 16 Bears, was credited with the win.

Sherm Lollar put the icing on the cake at the end of the Orioles first week in their new home. He hit four home runs (two in each game) as the Orioles swept the Toronto Maple Leafs in a doubleheader, 3-1 and 6-0.

THE 1944 ORIOLES

★

BACK ROW (L TO R): FRED PFEIFER, BATBOY RUSSELL HENDERSON, GEORGE SHAEFER,

AMBROSE PALICA, ROLLIE VAN SLATE, SHERMAN LOLLAR, BLAS MONACO.

MIDDLE ROW: KEN BRAUN, STAN WEST, HARRY IMHOFF, RED EMBREE, FRANK SKAFF, GEORGE HOOKS, SAM LOWRY,

FRANK ROCHEVOT, JOHN PODGAJNY, FELIX MACKIEWICZ, TRAINER EDDIE WEIDNER.

FRONT ROW: HOWIE MOSS, PAT RILEY, MILT STOCKHAUSEN, HAL KLEINE, MANAGER TOMMY THOMAS,

STAN BENJAMIN, BOB LATSHAW, LOU KAHN.

(LEFT TO RIGHT) BLAS MONACO, 2B; PAT RILEY, LF; STAN BENJAMIN, 3B;
FRANK SKAFF, SS; BOB LATSHAW, 1B; FELIX MACKIEWIEZ, CF;
HOWIE MOSS, RF; SHERMAN LOLLAR, C; ROLLAND VAN SLATE, PITCHER.

★

From Sunday to Sunday, the Orioles had won nine of 10 games, had attracted a record 63,500 fans, and re-captured first place with a 51-39 record.

As Paul Menton, veteran sports editor of the Baltimore Evening Sun, wrote: "You must go back to the years of Jack Dunn's pennant-winning years to find a comparative period of exciting and interesting baseball days like the past week since the Orioles made their debut in the stadium."

But, if Orioles fans thought the first week at the Stadium was fantastic, the next two weeks of that long homestand made them delirious.

After dispatching Toronto again, the Orioles met and swept the Montreal Royals in four straight double-headers. That's right, the Orioles won four double-headers on consecutive days.

By the time Montreal crawled out of town, the Orioles had won 18 of the first 19 games played at the Stadium. At 60-39 they were 6 1/2 games ahead of 2nd place Newark.

With the victory streak at 12, Baltimore next hosted last place Rochester in the fifth of six straight doubleheaders. Lefthander Hal Keine ran the streak to 13 in the opener, but in the nightcap, the Red Wings' Glenn Gardner halted the Orioles, 3-1, the lone Baltimore run scoring on a home run by Frank Skaff.

A CROWD OF NEARLY
33,000 FOR A 1ST
ROUND PLAYOFF GAME
AGAINST BUFFALO.

★

The next night the Orioles played their 6th consecutive twin bill and split (with Rochester) before rain washed out the series finale. Buffalo then moved into town to close out the marathon three-week homestand with a four-game series. The Orioles won the opener, but Buffalo prevailed in the final three games.

The remarkable stand closed with the Orioles going 21-6 while attracting 167,000 fans. They sported a record of 63-44 plus a 3 1/2 game lead over Newark. For the next five weeks the two clubs took turns grabbing the league lead. Then it all came down to the final day of the season with Newark holding a one-game lead.

The Orioles won the International League pennant in Jersey City that afternoon on the final day of the most exciting race in many seasons by splitting a double-header with the Jersey City Giants while the last place Syracuse Chiefs were defeating the Newark Bears in both ends of a twin bill. Baltimore won the league title by a margin of .0007.

The Birds won the first game, 5-0, behind the three-hit pitching of Red Embree, but lost the second game, 6-2. Newark was beaten, 4-1 and 4-3. The final standings show Baltimore at 84-68—.5526. Newark closed at 85-69—.5519.

It was Baltimore's first pennant since 1925 (the

last of their seven straight titles under Owner-Manager Jack Dunn).

Following the script that produced the regular season title as well as a victory over Buffalo in the first round of the playoffs, the Orioles used the entire seven games before eliminating the Newark Bears for the title.

It marked only the fourth time in International League history that the pennant-winning team had captured the playoffs.

Stan West went the distance and got offensive support from Sherm Lollar, Stan Benjamin and Kenny Braun who hit home runs during a 10-hit barrage against Don Johnson and Frank Hiller. The final score was 6-3.

Baltimore next took aim at the Junior World Series. A victory over Louisville would give the Orioles the "Grand Slam." It was a rare enough occurrence, and hadn't been accomplished since the Newark Bears had done it in 1938.

The first three games of the series were played in Louisville where a total of 33,786 Kentuckians

INSTALLING LIGHTS AT
MUNICIPAL STADIUM
FOR BASEBALL.

★

passed through the turnstiles to watch the Orioles win twice.

Louisville won the opener, 5-3, behind the five-hit pitching of Jim Wilson, the Colonels' ace who would pitch for the American League Orioles 11 years later. The Orioles rebounded to win the next two games, 11-0 and 7-4, before heading home.

The homecoming on October 9 was of record proportions. The Cardinals and Browns played the 6th game of the World Series that afternoon in front of a crowd of 31,630. That evening 52,833 poured out in Baltimore to watch the Orioles zdrop a 5-4 decision to the Colonels. It was a minor league record crowd and a total that the big league Orioles didn't surpass until 1966.

The next night the Orioles walloped the Colonels, 10-0, before 19,463 and closed out the series with a 5-3 victory as 23,536 joyous Baltimore fans looked on. The three games in Baltimore had drawn 95,882.

When all the attendance figures were tallied it came as no surprise that Baltimore had outdrawn

★
THE INTERNATIONAL
LEAGUE ORIOLES
CONTINUED TO PLAY ON
THE SAME SITE WHILE THE
NEW STADIUM WAS BEING
CONSTRUCTED.

most of the cities in the major leagues. More than 600,000 fans passed through the turnstiles.

The city's chances of securing a major league franchise brightened. Praises came from many prominent politicians, businessmen and writers—even the famous Grantland Rice. The man who made legends of the Four Horsemen of Notre Dame and labeled Red Grange as the Galloping Ghost, put his personal stamp of approval on Baltimore.

In a column at the conclusion of the Junior World Series, Rice wrote: "What are big league and what are minor league cities?

"The situation today is something of a joke. While the Cardinals and Browns were playing a World Series game before a less-than capacity 31,630 spectators, Baltimore and Louisville, two so-called minor league teams, were playing to 52,833 fans in Baltimore in a Junior World Series contest.

"Baltimore has no big-league team and St. Louis has two. Baltimore will draw 60,000 for any Navy-Notre Dame football game. It will draw close to 40,000 for any good pro football game.

"Baltimore is a stronger sporting center than St. Louis, but has no big league club, while St. Louis has two. If this is to be continued suppose we drop the names major and minor leagues. It doesn't make any sense.

"The time isn't very far away when you'll see a very decided change—or a big revolt against the present senseless system. This can't go on forever."

It didn't. Within the next decade Baltimore would become a major league city in three sports - basketball, football and baseball. The city entered the National Basketball League (a predecessor of the NBA) in 1947, joined the National Football League in 1950 (after three successful seasons in the ill-fated All-America Conference), then in 1954 re-joined the American League, after an absence of 52 years when the Browns relocated from St. Louis in what was the first franchise shift in American League baseball since the Orioles moved to New York in 1902 to become, ultimately, the New York Yankees.

★

MUNICIPAL STADIUM DURING THE 1944 LITTLE WORLD SERIES. ON OCT 9, A CROWD OF 52,833 SHOWED UP TO WATCH LOUISVILLE BEAT THE O'S AND TO SET AN ALL-TIME MINOR LEAGUE ATTENDANCE MARK. NOT TO WORRY, THE ORIOLES WON THE NEXT TWO GAMES TO CAPTURE THE SERIES.

16047

THE Great Ballpark Controversy

BY JOHN STEADMAN

It developed into a one-man crusade for Sports Editor Rodger H. Pippen. When the Junior Association of Commerce, strangely enough, took a public stance opposing the bond issue that would finance the new ballpark project, Pippen, who had been writing sports for the Baltimore News-Post for nearly half-a-century, reacted with his typical emotional fire. "It's a group," he wrote about the JAC, "whose accomplishments are known to neither man nor beast."

It was Pippen versus Mayor Thomas D'Alesandro Jr; director of public works Paul Holland; contractor Joseph Hughes; business leader Charles P. McCormick; aircraft building pioneer Glenn L. Martin and anyone else who, in Pippen's mind, was getting in the way of his own personal vision for a new ballpark in Baltimore.

It wasn't that Messrs. D'Alesandro, Holland, Hughes, McCormick and Martin opposed the concept of a new stadium, it was that they didn't

necessarily agree with all of Pippen's ideas on an issue that became an obsession.

The Sunpapers also differed with Pippen on the new ballpark, kindling another feud. During the ensuing battle, he frequently referred in print to The Morning Sun as "The Morning Wet Towel" and The Evening Sun as "The Evening Bologna." The whole idea of a sports editor attacking the rival newspaper wasn't considered the professional thing to do, but Pippen didn't care. At times it made for wonderful off-beat entertainment, but it ultimately became a tiring tirade, often testing the reader's tolerance to the breaking point.

Actually, the issue of a new stadium was not something Pippen planned to pursue in the beginning. In 1945 and 1946 he started with an entirely different objective: to put a cover over the old one. As the Orioles of the International League set attendance records in what was known as Municipal Stadium, a converted football horseshoe, fans

THE STADIUM BEGINS TO TAKE SHAPE. A MODERN STEEL AND CONCRETE FACILITY HAS, AT LAST, REPLACED THE OLD WOODEN STRUCTURE ON THE SAME LOCATION. THE YEAR IS 1953.

★

experienced severe discomfort whenever the weather was extreme. If it rained they got wet; on hot, humid Sunday afternoons, they could only sit there and swelter under the searing sun.

The campaign bore the title "We Want A Roof," and he was joined by some of his close friends. They began to collect signatures in on-the-street solicitations favoring the Pippen proposal. Soon Pippen's column and adjoining portions of the sports pages were packed with hundreds, then thousands, of names of those who were behind him in his quest to put a cover over the stadium's suffering spectators.

Truthfully, it would have been a travesty to spend money for a roof over a deteriorating stadium, where the exposed wooden benches had a life expectancy of about three years before requiring repair or replacement.

But, gradually, as the "roof" campaign wore on, Pippen developed the feeling that Baltimore had a chance to get major league baseball. In the early stages of the new stadium game, his was the only voice being heard. Some said it was a pipe-dream and others thought Pippen, who had as many detractors as supporters, was just creating commotion.

However, some credence was given the effort after Clark Griffith, owner of the Washington Senators and a close friend, told Pippen he would "give" him his vote to approve Baltimore if the American League addressed the matter. Griffith, furthermore, put the promise in writing. This was an important development.

So Pippen was carrying on still another battle. He got the attention of politicians, the public and even the

★

PUBLISHER FRED I. ARCHIBALD PRESENTS RODGER H. PIPPEN A PLAQUE ON HIS RETIREMENT IN 1958. JOE TIPMAN, FORMER BOXER, IS ON RIGHT.

Sunpapers. The chances of wooing major league baseball back to this city were slim, roof or no roof, if the team would have to play in the old stadium. He hammered away ad nauseam in advocating the construction of a modern facility to replace the antiquated stadium that had been in place since 1922.

In 1947, a bond vote was approved by city constituents for $2,500,000. But, that wasn't enough to complete the job, and a similar request was made in 1948. The Sunpapers advised their readers to vote against it, and it was narrowly defeated (against: 78,012, for: 73,014). That defeat only inspired Pippen to fire more punches.

He dredged up some 34-year-old material when he accused the Sun of "driving Babe Ruth out of Baltimore." His explanation for that allegation was that their editors in 1914 devoted prime space to Baltimore's Terrapins of the Federal League, the so-called major league, while neglecting the International League Orioles, owned by Jack Dunn. The low gate receipts that followed, Pippen insisted, forced Dunn to sell Babe Ruth, his fabulous rookie pitcher, to the Boston Red Sox to get badly-needed operating funds.

But over three decades later, the city had developed considerable interest in securing a major league franchise, and decided to spend the first $2,500,000 to build a partial stadium, hoping another loan would still be possible. The bond issue was presented again in 1950 and Pippen kept pounding away. This time the Sunpapers, on their sample ballot, left the question open, advising voters to decide for themselves. And, decide they did, in favor by a substantial margin (89,970 to 64,320). Baltimore was on its way to the big leagues.

★

IT'S TIME FOR A CELEBRATION. AND CITY HALL IS BEDECKED IN BUNTING TO MARK ORIOLES RETURN TO THE MAJOR LEAGUES.

★

HOW TO BUILD A BALLPARK WHILE THE TEAM IS STILL PLAYING. AERIAL VIEW
PROVIDES GRAPHIC LOOK AT OLD CONFIGURATION WHILE CONSTRUCTION
PROGRESSES IN ANOTHER PART OF THE STADIUM IN THE LATE 1940S.

Mayor D'Alesandro, by this time, was firmly in the big league baseball corner, too. But Jesse A. Linthicum, sports editor of The Morning Sun, made light of the possibility. He enjoyed irritating Pippen by writing, "At a late hour last night, the Browns were still in St. Louis." The last time he wrote those taunting words was on the morning before the Browns came to Baltimore.

Pippen was pleased with the victory, but it had been a tiring and troublesome eight year struggle. Perhaps, Baltimore's return to the American League would have happened eventually, but Pippen's role certainly facilitated the final result.

Even his enemies, and they were numerous, could not deny or minimize the effectiveness of his fight. To show that they held no animosity, for example, The Sun later recognized its old antagonizer's achievements by including Pippen among the handful of people who had made a lasting impact on, and contribution to, Baltimore sports during the first 150 years of its publishing life.

Stadium Diagrams

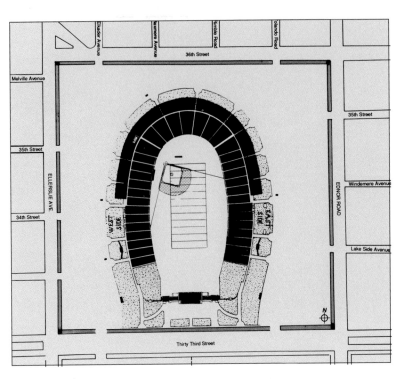

Municipal Stadium

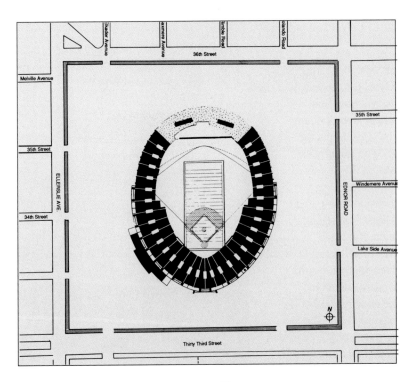

Memorial Stadium

THE Seven-Month Miracle

BY JOHN STEADMAN

BALTIMORE'S ORIGINAL STADIUM

Decisions—in war as in peace—often take on more importance with the passing of time, resulting in a telling impact on history. That's what transpired in 1922 when Mayor William Broening said he wanted to build a stadium. His wish, as incredulous as it then seemed, became an almost instant command. With little discussion and a minimum of debate, it happened.

The stadium was created on the same property where Memorial Stadium, which replaced it, now stands. But keep in mind the expediency with which it all originally occurred. In November of 1921, the mayor made the pronouncement Baltimore was in need of an outdoor amphitheater, or stadium, to hold major college football games and, hopefully, to eventually regain a major league baseball franchise.

Five months later the site was selected and, after seven more months, the facility was completed and opened for its first event—a football game between the Army 3rd Corps Area and the Quantico Marines. The speed with which it all happened

THE CORPS OF CADETS MARCHING AT MUNICIPAL STADIUM ON THE DAY OF THE ARMY-NAVY GAME IN 1924.

★

shows that Broening operated at a time when bureaucracy was subservient to the personal dictates of the mayor.

Broening, thus, is the godfather of Baltimore sports. Without that facility, the city would have had no chance to recover its big league status. In 1921, alumni of Johns Hopkins University seriously discussed enlarging its campus stadium, Homewood Field. But the city quickly moved ahead of the Hopkins' planners and pre-empted the effort before it gained momentum.

That Broening picked an undeveloped area, then known as Venable Park, for the Stadium was one of the great upsets in political decision-making. Most of the public sentiment in 1922 concentrated on other locations: The abandoned Mt. Royal Reservoir at North and Mt. Royal Avenues; the open space of Clifton Park, near where a junior high school was later erected; Druid Hill Park, Wyman Park, Walbrook Oval, Stoney Run Valley, the Seminary of St. Sulpice on Paca Street; and two historic locales, Fort McHenry and Federal Hill.

Venable Park was on land owned by the city, surrounded by attractive new housing developments created by Baltimore builders Frank Novak on the east and E. J. Gallagher on the west. It was Baltimore's hope to have a stadium that would rival

MAYOR WILLIAM F. BROENING SPEARHEADED THE PROJECT. IN THIS PHOTO, MAYOR BROENING IS WEARING HIS ORIOLES CAP WHILE PARTICIPATING IN SPECIAL CEREMONIES AT OLD ORIOLE PARK.

★

the Yale Bowl, put up in 1921; Harvard Stadium, which dated to 1903; or Archbold Stadium at Syracuse University, built in 1907.

Meanwhile, the New York Yankees were going on their own, after leaving the Polo Grounds, to construct Yankee Stadium, which officially began on May 6, only three days before the groundbreaking in Baltimore. The proceedings here were marked by Theodore Mottu of the Park Board swinging the first pick and Mayor Broening lifting the ceremonial shovel for what became an excavation and movement of 200,000 yards of earth to develop the stadium.

Steam shovels and 200 laborers, along with mules and wagons, shoved the dirt into huge embankments while a grader leveled the playing field. Then planks were placed on three earthen sides to provide seating. Only a limited space was placed in concrete, down front, where folding chairs could be set up to accomodate the distinguished guests. For the most part, the seats were buttock against raw wood, offering little comfort. With exposure to the weather, the deterioration of the bleacher-type seats soon became an ongoing problem, where splinters in the posterior often necessitated visits to the first-aid stations on game days for emergency "surgery."

The official unveiling of the stadium, on December 2, 1922, was a well-planned public spectacle. It was the largest crowd to assemble in Baltimore since the 1912 Democratic Convention nominated Woodrow Wilson. The stadium opened to a football game between two military teams, not to be confused with the Army-Navy classic. The game featured the Army's 3rd Corps Area against the Quantico Marines.

Only a year earlier the same two teams played at Homewood Field where the Army lost, 20-0. It was to be a rare defeat for the coach of the Army team. He was to become supreme commander of the Allied Expeditionary Force in World War II, and later the country's 34th president, Dwight D. Eisenhower. When Venable Stadium opened, however, Eisenhower had been assigned elsewhere, thus depriving Baltimore of an important and historic footnote.

The pomp and ceremony accompanying the inaugural event was spectacular. A parade from Mount Royal Railroad Station to the stadium included close to 12,000 soldiers and marines, led by the famed City Troop of Philadelphia, organized in 1775.

Three Cabinet members were present: Edward Denby, Secretary of the Navy; John Weeks, Secretary of War; and James Davis, Secretary of Labor. So were the governors of three states, Albert Ritchie of Maryland, William Sproul of Pennsylvania, and Lee Trinkle of Virginia. A 21-gun salute highlighted the pre-game dedication ceremonies.

There was good-natured jeering and cheering between the rooting sections. The Army crowd began to chant to the Marines, nicknamed the Leathernecks, "Go Wash Your Necks...Go Wash Your Necks." The Army mule was on hand. So was the Marine mascot, a bulldog wearing a tin helmet.

As the game commenced, a Marine sergeant talked into what was described as a radio telephone to the White House, where President Warren G. Harding and his wife, Florence, listened to the sergeant's make shift play-by-play. A chorus sang the "First Lady's" favorite song, "The End of a Perfect Day." When Mrs. Harding was asked about the reception, she said, "Fine. We can hear everything, and it's great."

Although the two teams were in the main comprised of enlisted men, there were some former West Point and Naval Academy football players, newly commissioned officers, in both lineups. For historical purposes the first points, a drop kick field

★
THE GRAND OPENING—
DECEMBER 2, 1922—
QUANTICO MARINES 13,
U.S. ARMY 3RD CORPS 12.
ESTIMATED ATTENDANCE:
50,000.

OPENING GAME
ARMY VS. MARINES
DECEMBER 2, 1922
ATTENDANCE 50,000

"THE GRAND CANYON"
HERE'S HOW THIS MASSIVE PROJECT LOOKED DURING CONSTRUCTION.

★

goal, were scored by Gene Vidal of the Army in a contest that was won 13-12 by the Marines. The initial event was an overwhelming success, attended by famed sports writer Walter Camp, regarded as one of the fathers of American college football. The Baltimore Sun had its sports writers covering the game, but engaged W. W. (Bill) Roper, the illustrious Princeton coach, to provide a technical analysis.

The lead story on Page One of the Sun was by Raymond S. Tompkins, who called on dramatic emotion. His lead follows:

"United States Marines, fighting by land and air, beat the United States Army, 13-12, at football yesterday in Venable Stadium, Baltimore's mighty outdoor arena.

"It was a new stadium, dedicated just before the game. The crowd of more than 50,000 people, who sat and stood in and around it, was seeing it in use for the first time.

"It is not a new Stadium now. It has lived and suffered, if a giant of concrete and earth can do that. It knows the blackest depths of despair and the most golden heights of triumph.

"It must be a good Stadium. It was still there last night, a ghostly moonlit playground for witches, perhaps, after a day of pageantry, splendor and joyous tumult, ending with a struggle that should have rocked a mountain."

J. Cookman Boyd, president of the Park Board, who was instrumental in implementing the desires of Mayor Broening by making the Stadium a reality, gave a personal accounting of the size of the crowd: 43,034 in permanent seats; 10,000 standing along the sidelines; and 7,000 clamoring outside, peering in, for a distant look at the game.

In two years, the seating capacity of Venable Stadium was to be virtually doubled, which enabled Baltimore to host the Army-Navy game in 1924. But in 1922, the grand opener was a momentous social as well as athletic occasion. Counted in the crowd for the Quantico-3rd Corps encounter was the West Point coaching staff of head coach Charles Daly and assistant Major R. R. Bob Neyland, who later became a Hall of Fame coach at Tennessee; Major F. H. O'Hara and Captain J. F. McEwan. Also with the Army delegation was Matthew B. Ridgway, the athletic director, who covered himself with battlefield glory in World

War II as leader of the 82nd Airborne.

And, oh, yes, in 1922 it was important to make sure there would be no drinking in the new Venable Stadium. Eight agents of the Maryland Prohibition Commission (MPC) were there to guard against violators of the Volstead Act. The Commissioner of the MPC, Edmund Budnitz, an attorney and the grandfather of the later Johns Hopkins University Lacrosse All-America, was in attendance as a football enthusiast and didn't intend to assert his authority, unless an emergency arose.

Physically, the stadium was awesome in size. To look down from any seat in the horseshoe configuration, this sprawling pile of lumber, so to speak, suggested the vastness of a huge cavern. Over 200,000 yards of earth had been excavated and deposited on each side of the playing field and behind one end zone. About 500,000 board feet measure of lumber, nothing sophisticated, was used to build the plank seats with a projected life of three to five years.

The field itself measured 960' by 357' and covered an area of seven acres, while the entire stadium encompassed 20 acres.

The total construction period consumed a little less than seven months from ground-breaking to completion. Much credit was heaped on the Park Board, including J. Cookman Boyd, president, and Theodore Mottu, Gen. Felix Angus and Edward Hanlon, plus Henry G. Perring, the city's chief engineer, for carrying the project to such a rapid conclusion. Total cost: $458,000, which tells us that dollars for a stadium stretched farther in those happy, carefree days after World War I.

Baltimore then had little grasp of what the stadium was going to mean in shaping its sports future. It was, indeed, the key to eventually opening the door to major league baseball and football.

The Orioles, after being burned out of their Oriole Park bandbox, moved there in 1944, and it was there that the Colts established residence in 1947. Make no mistake about it, the availability of the old stadium was absolutely essential to making Baltimore's major league dream come true.

THE BALTIMORE STADIUM ADMINISTRATION BUILDING FACING 33RD STREET. THE STADIUM AT DIFFERENT TIMES ALSO WAS KNOWN AS MUNICIPAL, VENABLE, BABE RUTH, AND, IN 1950, MEMORIAL STADIUM, THE NAME THE NEW BALLPARK THAT REPLACED IT IN 1954 HAS ALWAYS WORN.

*

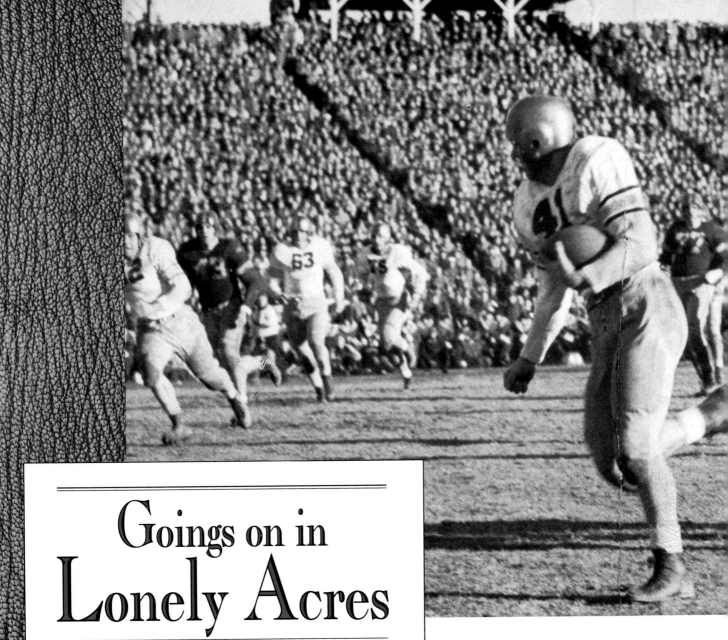

Goings on in Lonely Acres

BY JOHN STEADMAN

Before the Baltimore Orioles found an emergency home in Municipal Stadium in July 1944, after Oriole Park went up in flames, the facility was continually demeaned by critics. "Lonely Acres" they called it because it seemed to be vacant more than it had a right to be.

The Orioles had their own ballpark, were contented members of the International League, and didn't require more than the 12,000 seats their compact baseball facility offered.

In the early life of the stadium, there were three particularly momentous highlights: the Army-Navy games in 1924 and 1944, and the Little World Series between the Orioles and American Association champion Louisville Colonels, also in 1944.

Army-Navy in 1924 packed a crowd of 80,000,

including President and Mrs. Calvin Coolidge, into the then two-year-old plant. It was an unusual game in that center and team captain Ed Garbisch tried seven drop-kick field goals and made four of them, all in the second half, for a 12-0 Army victory. The drop kick has become passe since then and games in which all the scoring is produced by field goals are exceedingly rare.

A 20-year wait ensued before another Army-Navy game came Baltimore's way, in the midst of World War II, and it happened without expectation.

The 1944 game was supposed to be played at tiny Thompson Field in Annapolis, but was transferred to Baltimore because both teams were as powerful as any in the nation. Public interest called for the change, with approval from President Franklin Roosevelt.

It was also suggested that an enormous amount of money might be raised for the war effort by

playing the game in Baltimore Stadium. It was a colossal meeting as Glenn Davis and Felix (Doc) Blanchard, two subsequent winners of the Heisman Trophy, led the Army charge in a 23-7 triumph. Navy countered with such brilliant performers as Don Whitmire, Ben Chase, Dick Duden, Clyde (Smackover) Scott and Hal Hamberg.

Then and now, in retrospect, it was considered the most important sports event to occur in this country during World War II. Army's victory made it the uncontested national champion.

What made this game different than any other in history was the way tickets were sold. Before you could order a ticket, it was necessary to purchase a war bond. The larger the bond, the better the seat location. A record $58,638,000 in war bonds were sold, the biggest one-day bond sale during all of World War II.

The West Point cadets came to Baltimore, under unusual and secret travel arrangements, imposed by war-time censorship and security. Trains and busses were not available for such frivolous pursuits. They were being utilized to move troops and supplies. On game day, the Corps of Cadets, after arriving, seemingly out of nowhere, on a troopship in the inner harbor, marched as the "Long Gray Line" through the streets of Baltimore on their way to the climactic showdown with Navy that attracted 70,000, including General

MUNICIPAL STADIUM DURING THE 1944
ARMY-NAVY GAME THAT SETTLED THE
NATIONAL CHAMPIONSHIP.

★

George C. Marshall and Admiral W.D. Leahy.

It wasn't until after the war that a New York newspaperman, Harold Rosenthal, revealed the logistics behind the Cadets journey from West Point to Baltimore. They had boarded, under the veil of war-time secrecy, a transport that carried them down the Hudson River, hugged the Atlantic Coast past New Jersey, Delaware and Maryland, then turned up the Chesapeake Bay and on into Baltimore.

In that same year, 1944, the Orioles, playing to a large number of service personnel and war plant employees, stationed or working in the area, found the stadium a place of magic. Crowds in excess of 20,000, 30,000 and 40,000 to see minor league baseball caught the attention of the nation. Clark Griffith, owner of the Washington Senators, couldn't believe the newspaper figures and often called to verify the attendance counts with Herb Armstrong, the Orioles' business manager. The 52,833 for a Little World Series game against Louisville served as a catalyst for Baltimore's ultimate return to the major leagues.

If the facility was largely underused from the time it opened in 1922 until the American League Orioles moved into the rebuilt facility in 1954, it was nevertheless the scene of a wide and varied agenda of public events.

There was the annual Firemen-Marine football game when the City Fire Department took on the Quantico Marines. It was generally a mismatch, but when the two combatants played baseball at Oriole Park, come summertime, the "Smokeaters" would get even with the "Leathernecks," as the sports writers were fond of putting it.

Joe Louis, one of the greatest of boxing champions, had a 10-round bout there with Jimmy Bivins in 1951, prior to being knocked out two months later by Rocky Marciano. A polo match played for the Damon Runyon Cancer Fund, and sponsored by the Baltimore News-Post, drew what

Y GAME
STADIUM
, 1924

ARMY VS. NAVY
NOVEMBER 29, 1924
LARGEST FOOTBALL ATTENDANCE
AT BALTIMORE STADIUM -
80,150

qualified as a then world record polo crowd of 20,000. After the game a park board official asked Mayor Thomas D'Alesandro Jr., for an emergency appropriation to resod the field. D'Alesandro didn't understand. It was explained the polo ponies had torn up the turf. The mayor, who only cared about baseball and bocce, asked incredulously: "Who gave 'em permission to use horses?"

The stadium was a catch-all for promoters, who seemed to stay up late, trying to think of what they might offer to attract ticket buyers and, thus, turn a dollar for themselves. It was a time when Baltimore was often dismissed as a "whistle stop" between Washington and Philadelphia. Baltimore, for the most part, was in the national sports focus only twice a year—in the spring for the Preakness, and in the fall for the Navy-Notre Dame game when it was scheduled here.

"Sleepy" old Baltimore was to come alive, and the part played by sports in general, and the Naval Academy in particular, in bringing about the metamorphosis, can never be denied. A Navy game with any foe took on a luster that no other college teams could offer. Seeing the brigade of Midshipmen march from Clifton Park to Memorial Stadium, up Alameda Boulevard to 33rd Street and through the massive stadium gates, on both sides of

IMMORTAL HEAVYWEIGHT CHAMPION JOE LOUIS FOUGHT A 10 ROUND BOUT AGAINST JIMMY BIVINS AT THE STADIUM IN 1951.

★

the administration building, became an integral part of the pre-kickoff ceremonies.

It was such an impressive display that men, women and children, even those uninterested in football, would line the nearby sidewalks to observe the precision marching and listen to the Naval Academy band. Navy made its first football appearance at the Stadium in 1923, a year after the opening, when it hosted Princeton which had a large Baltimore alumni contingent. The game resulted in a 3-3 tie before a crowd of 45,000.

The Baltimore Park Board realized early that Navy was an excellent drawing magnet. Over the years, until a regrettable incident occurred involving Baltimore Colts owner Caroll Rosenbloom in the mid-1950s, the Navy found Baltimore an enjoyable and profitable place to play. Rosenbloom deliberately ignored a Park Board-Naval Academy agreement, and the Navy quietly went elsewhere.

A superb mix of visiting college teams came to

Baltimore to play Navy for over four decades, including appearances by Ohio State, Michigan, California, Princeton, Notre Dame, North Carolina, Cornell, Columbia, Penn State, Yale, Harvard, Dartmouth, Georgia Tech, Southern California, Tulane and Northwestern. Navy was considered a major power and, in 1923, even received a bid to play the University of Washington in the Rose Bowl.

Maryland and Western Maryland, which enjoyed extraordinary success under coach Dick Harlow, and gained top-20 ranking, also booked dates in the Stadium. In 1932, what turned into the first North-South All-Star game was played there. It was an attempt by Baltimore to get into the bowl game madness, but a blizzard hit the city, wiping out the yard lines and holding the crowd to a mere 1,723. Subsequently the concept found a more suitable clime in Miami's Orange Bowl.

The historic first Notre Dame-Navy game was played in Baltimore. It was 1927 and the series, which opened with a handshake agreement between Irish Coach Knute Rockne and the Midshipmen's Bill Ingram, was the start of what, to this day, remains the longest uninterrupted intersectional rivalry in the country. That first game in the series and others to follow drew on ethnic interest, as represented by the large Irish Catholic population in Baltimore. The game provided classic overtones during an interval when Baltimore didn't offer much else of major league appeal.

At that first game in 1927, General Douglas MacArthur, then head of the Army's 3rd Corps Area, was present as an interested spectator. It was the same MacArthur, who, after the Army-Navy game of 1944, also played in Baltimore, sent an emotional cable from his Pacific Headquarters to Earl (Red) Blaik, coach of the winning Cadets. It read, "To the greatest of all Army teams. We have

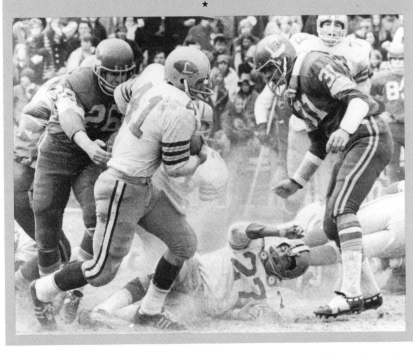

THE CITY-POLY AND LOYOLA-CALVERT HALL FOOTBALL RIVALRIES WERE RENEWED ANNUALLY AT MUNICIPAL STADIUM, A TRADITION THAT CONTINUES EVERY THANKSGIVING DAY AT MEMORIAL STADIUM.

★

★
GENERAL
DOUGLAS MACARTHUR

★
COLONEL
CHARLES LINDBERGH.

stopped the war to celebrate your magnificent success." A dramatic overstatement, but typical of MacArthur's extraordinary eloquence. Blaik later said that victory and MacArthur's congratulations represented his most rewarding moment in a sterling coaching career.

The Notre Dame debut in Baltimore was the beginning of what evolved into a policy of playing here almost every other season.

The stadium, over the years, became virtually an all-purpose facility though, in the main, it was known as a football arena. It was there that the City-Poly, and, much later, the Loyola-Calvert Hall games were played (a tradition that continues every Thanksgiving Day at Memorial Stadium).

Always in need of events, it was at the Stadium that Charles Lindbergh appeared for a hero's welcome after becoming the first to fly solo across the Atlantic Ocean in 1927. Lindbergh's arrival, following a parade, was held in early October, five months after the flight, and it drew 20,000 in a driving rain.

The Stadium also hosted on various occasions: the aforementioned polo match; midget automobile races; Lucky Teeter Daredevil Auto Shows; rodeos (with an invitation to ride a powerful bull named "Big Sid"); boxing matches; Easter Sunrise religious rites; July Fourth Fireworks extravaganzas; firemen-police-postal service track meets, and the North-South Lacrosse all-star game. It also served as a staging area for a divergent array of public assemblies.

In a way, the Stadium became the Town Hall of Baltimore. And, "Lonely Acres" or not, Baltimore would not be the big league town it is today had Mayor Broening not ordered its construction nearly 70 years ago. And it all came about in only seven months time.

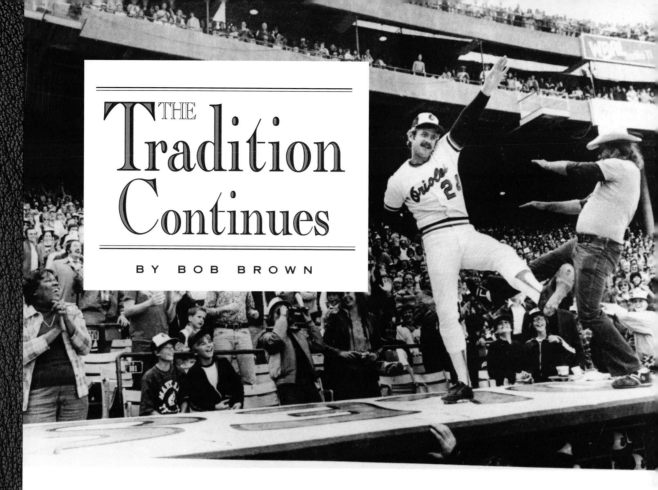

THE Tradition Continues

BY BOB BROWN

RICK DEMPSEY AND WILD BILL HAGY
CUTTIN' UP ON THE DUGOUT.

★

In the mid-seventies Frank Cashen returned to the beer business (albeit briefly), and he was replaced as general manager by Hank Peters. Almost without skipping a beat, the Orioles went on to enjoy another stretch of extended success. They were solid contenders for a division championship in seven of nine seasons from '75 thru '83 and finished first or second eight times.

If the personnel, the victory totals and the frequency of championships were not quite up to the standard set between '66 and '74, the Orioles of the latter era were, certainly, better appreciated than their predecessors.

The grand old game's national renaissance didn't really reach Baltimore until well after the juggernaut of '69-'70-'71 had been broken up. Those three straight 100-victory teams never experienced the consistent enthusiasm and adulation that greeted both the game, itself, and those who played it professionally here in Birdland later in the decade, and beyond.

Young people, absent in droves for

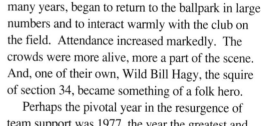

many years, began to return to the ballpark in large numbers and to interact warmly with the club on the field. Attendance increased markedly. The crowds were more alive, more a part of the scene. And, one of their own, Wild Bill Hagy, the squire of section 34, became something of a folk hero.

Perhaps the pivotal year in the resurgence of team support was 1977, the year the greatest and most beloved of all Orioles removed his cape for the last time.

He was no longer a regular by this time, and candidly admitted that he felt more comfortable not playing. But, early on he found one last longball in his bat, and although there weren't many at the ballpark for that wonderful moment, it was no less dramatic. The paid attendance for that cool, damp April 19 night game in 1977 was a sparse 4,826 and when the Indians went ahead 5-2 in the top of the 10th off Tippy Martinez and Dyar Miller, many of them

WHAT A RIDE IT HAD BEEN.

★

checked out.

With Dave LaRoche pitching for Cleveland in the bottom of the 10th, the Birds got something going. Lee May drove in a run to make it 5-3 and with two on and one out, Brooks came out of the dugout to bat for Larry Harlow.

GLEN BURNIE'S JOHN STEFERO BURNED THE BREWERS TWO NIGHTS IN A ROW.
★

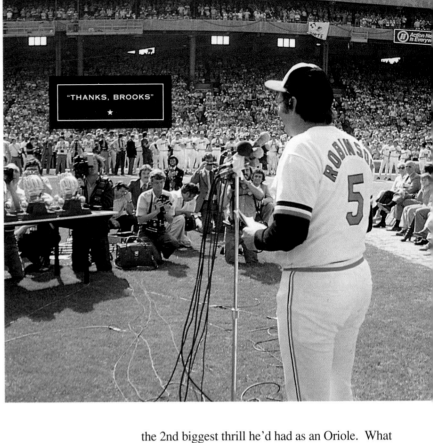

He fouled off some tough pitches, eventually worked the count to 3-2, and then hit a drive to left field. It wasn't a tape measure blast and there was some question whether it had enough distance. For a moment there was some serious praying going on among the hometown fans, but the ball slipped into the bleachers, and the loyal little band went into a frenzy of joy. It wasn't just the Orioles had won a game in exciting style, it was that Brooksie had won it, just as he'd done so many times before. It was just like the good old days.

In the Orioles clubhouse, there was World Series-like euphoria as media, players and staff alike surrounded the locker of everybody's favorite player. The skipper, Earl Weaver, all 5'8" of him wrapped up in one big smile, admitted that it was

★
THE ORIOLES CLUB-
HOUSE, THE IN PLACE
TO BE. AL BUMBRY,
JIM PALMER, TIPPY
MARTINEZ AND
ELLIE HENDRICKS.

the 2nd biggest thrill he'd had as an Oriole. What was his first? Well, Brooksie had a lot to say about that one, too. The 1970 World Series.

Five months later, the Orioles and their fans threw a party at the ballpark for the retiring third baseman. They called it "Thanks Brooks" Day. As you might suspect, the weather was perfect on that September Sunday afternoon and the ballpark was full. In fact, the crowd of 51,798 that poured into the ballpark that day was the largest for a regular season event the Orioles had ever drawn.

When the hour and a half ceremony concluded amid one last thunderous ovation for the Orioles' living legend, there was an important ballgame to play, the 2nd place Orioles and the 3rd place Red Sox, both just a few games back of the division leading Yankees. The Orioles lost that game, but nobody seemed to care a whole lot. This was a day for honoring Brooks, there'd be time to worry about wins and losses tomorrow.

There was a warm and wonderful bit of counter-point to this story in 1977. The 23-year veteran, enroute to the Hall of Fame, getting the last of many game-winning hits on the one hand; and the obscure little minor league catcher, brought up as an injury replacement, compacting a lifetime of memories into two glorious days in the big leagues.

His name was Dave Criscione, and there was something about him that turned on the Baltimore crowd. His wife gave birth to their first child on Thursday, and on Sunday (July 24) in the second game of a doubleheader sweep against the Brewers,

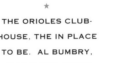

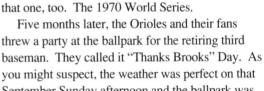

THE O'S GIVE THEIR FANS
A WELL DESERVED "O" OF
THEIR OWN.

he made his first (and only) start and picked up his first two big league hits, for both of which he drew standing ovations. In the 8th inning of that game, he earned still another ovation for successfully sacrificing the eventual winning run into scoring position.

He had already risen to the rank of "people's choice" in one afternoon, but there was more to come. The Birds played the Brewers again the next night and had them down 2-1 until Milwaukee's Lenn Sakata (his name will come up again in this piece) hit his first major league homer with a man aboard to put the Brewers ahead.

However, the O's tied it in their half and the score remained 3-3 into the 11th. Criscione had

entered late in the game after the starting catcher Dave Skaggs had been removed for a pinch-hitter, and up he strode to the plate with one out and none on. A few moments later. Boom! The ballgame was over. The people's choice had struck again. The crowd was delirious.

Dave Criscione never played in another game at Memorial Stadium and by August 10 was back in the minor leagues to stay. But not before he had etched his name permanently on the Orioles' list of legends.

Several years later, in

DOUG DECINCES' SUDDEN
DEATH HOME RUN THAT
FRIDAY NIGHT IN JUNE '79
SERVED AS A CATALYST
FOR ORIOLES FANS.

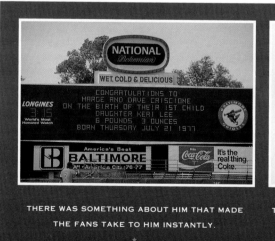

THERE WAS SOMETHING ABOUT HIM THAT MADE
THE FANS TAKE TO HIM INSTANTLY.

THE "PEOPLES CHOICE."
DAVE CRISCIONE.

'83, the Orioles had another catcher up from the minors who never achieved regular status, but still made a lasting contribution. He was a local youngster named John Stefero. In two games back-to-back against the Brewers here in mid-September, he delivered "sudden death" game-winning singles. To this day, the two unkindest words you can say to Brewers owner Bud Selig are "Criscione" and "Stefero."

The only year in this stretch when the Orioles didn't finish at least as high as 2nd was 1978, but that aberration was forgotten on or about June 22 the following year. The O's had jumped off to a good start and they were playing .667 (44-22) ball (Dennis Martinez was already 10-2) when they engaged the Tigers in a weekend series at home.

They were losing 4-3 in the 9th when with one down Ken Singleton homered, then Eddie Murray singled. One out later Doug DeCinces hit a game-winning homer off Detroit's Dave Tobik and that ballgame was history. It seems, even now, that the DeCinces blast served as a catalyst, if not for the Orioles who were already hot, then certainly for their fans. It

THE AL'S '80 CY YOUNG AWARD WINNER STEVE STONE (LEFT) DESCRIBED THE ORIOLES AS, "A WE TEAM, NOT AN I TEAM."

★

★

THE ORIOLES LOGGED 7 FIRSTS DURING JERRY HOFFBERGER'S 14 YEARS AS BOARD CHAIRMAN ('66 - '79).

made them believers, and the rest of the weekend merely fortified that new-found faith.

The next night in the first of a doubleheader, the Birds again trailed by one in the bottom of the 9th, until Eddie Murray smacked a 3-run homer off Detroit's ace reliever John Hiller. In the nightcap of that twin bill, it was a pinch-hit single in the bottom of the 8th by Terry Crowley that brought the Tigers to their knees and Orioles fans to their feet.

Earl Weaver bragged about his "deep depth," guys like Crowley, Pat Kelly, John Lowenstein, Gary Roenicke, and Benny Ayala and others who did so much damage coming off the bench. By mid-season righthander Steve Stone, in his first year here, had figured out how this club differed from the others he'd been with. He said, "This is a *WE* team, not an *I* team."

The Orioles were 31 games over .500 at Memorial Stadium (55-24) in 1979, and they attributed that hometown advantage in significant measure to the tremendous and heretofore unprecedented support of the folks in and around Birdland.

They weren't just blowing smoke. At the end of the final regular season game at the stadium on September 26, well after they'd clinched the division championship, the players, manager and coaches decided it was high time they saluted the fans. So out of the dugout they scrambled, some in uniform, some in street clothes, and produced their own O-R-I-O-L-E-S cheer for the folks in the seats.

It was a fitting and very emotional gesture. Afterward Ken Singleton, the Orioles MVP that season, described that magic moment eloquently: "We owed that to them, and much, much more. And, we realized that all of the people there tonight might not be at the playoff games.

"So we were saying thank you from us. And they were saying they'd be pulling for us whether they were in the park or not. It was a wonderful night to be a part of."

The next year, 1980, was almost as good. The O's won 100 games, only two fewer than the pennant-winning previous year, but finished second to the Yankees. There was one stretch in August

AT BAT	BALL	STRIKE	OUT	H-E	TIME
		2	2		7:48

CROWN GASOLINE *Seen Every Mile!*

	3	4	5	6	7	8	9	10	R	H	E	IG
	0	2	0	0	0	3	0		5	8	1	
	0	3	3	0	0	0			6	9	0	

253 636 FANS HERE THIS
---THANK YOU VERY MUCH

BUCKY DENT TAKES AN 0-2 PITCH FOR A CALLED STRIKE THREE AS THE O'S CAPTURED THE RUBBER GAME IN THE 5-GAME SERIES THAT DREW A MAJOR LEAGUE RECORD QUARTER OF A MILLION FANS (AUG '80).

when the Orioles played an amazing 11 straight games against first place teams (8 vs. the Yankees they were trying desperately to catch, and 3 against the Royals who led in the west).

It was during that period in August that the Orioles and the Yankees set an all-time major league record, drawing a quarter of a million people for a 5-game series (the official total was 249,605).

That was the year Steve Stone went 25-7, won the Cy Young and pitched three perfect innings as the American League starter in the All-Star Game.

It was also the season that John Lowenstein conned an entire ballpark full of fans one June night while producing one of those never to be forgotten Orioles moments.

Late one June night, Brother Lo drove in the tying run in the 8th inning with a single to right that

CAL JR. GETS PAT FROM HIS DAD ON THE OCCASION OF HIS FIRST BIG LEAGUE HOMER.

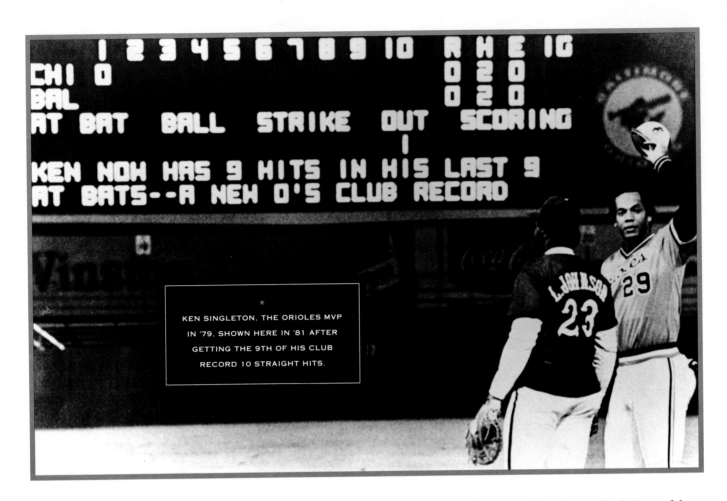

KEN SINGLETON, THE ORIOLES MVP IN '79, SHOWN HERE IN '81 AFTER GETTING THE 9TH OF HIS CLUB RECORD 10 STRAIGHT HITS.

also sent speedy Al Bumbry scooting from 1st to 3rd. Then as the rightfielder unleashed a throw to the plate, John broke for 2nd. The throw was cut off and relayed to 2nd in an attempt to nail Lowenstein. Nail him it did, in the back of the neck. The ball caromed into the outfield, Bumbry scampered home with what proved to be the winning run and all the home folks were happy.

Suddenly, however, joy turned to grief. Lowenstein was hurt. A stretcher was rushed out and as he was carried off the field, lying motionless, as if unconscious, the stands rocked with grim, sympathetic applause.

Moments later, applause gave way to laughter. The fans suddenly realized they'd been taken. Just before the stretcher disappeared down the dugout steps, on the way to the training room, John sat bolt upright and gave out with his best double-fisted salute. "I had it planned halfway to the dugout," he said later. "After all, we *were* on tv."

Forgettable is the best word to describe 1981. Labor difficulties took 8 1/2 weeks

EDDIE AND CAL, AN AWESOME 1-2 PUNCH.

(from June 11 until Aug 10) right out of the middle of it. That was the year of the infamous two half seasons. In all, the clubs played about two thirds of their games, and the Orioles didn't fare that badly. Their overall record (59-46) was only one game back of the best in the division (Milwaukee); yet the O's finished first in neither half (the Yankees and Brewers were the half-season winners).

In many ways the 1982 season, more specifically the last several weeks of it, was one of the Orioles' most memorable and satisfying despite the fact it did not yield a championship. Read Jim Henneman's stirring recollection of that rousing finish elsewhere on these pages, entitled "The Lost Weekend."

As it turned out the Orioles reached the end of an era in 1983, but what a way to go. It has been called alternately "The Year of Redemption," because it exorcized, at long last, the painful memories of past near misses (1971, 1980 and 1982); and "The Most Rewarding Year," because so many good things happened to this close-knit group of good guys.

Though the club had a new manager (Joe

Altobelli), the system operated essentially the same way it had under Earl Weaver. Probably because Earl's successor wasn't new at all. He was a longtime veteran of the Baltimore organization, who had been away for a few years, and was thoroughly familiar with what was called "The Oriole Way."

Young Cal Ripken won the MVP, a season after he'd been the league's top rookie, and for the first time ever, the Orioles topped 2,000,000 at the Memorial Stadium gate.

The O's didn't have what you could call a regular leftfielder that year (or the year before), they had a bunch of guys who took turns playing the position. John Lowenstein was one, Gary Roenicke another and Benny Ayala an occasional third. Together that coalition produced MVP stats. Only while playing left field, excluding appearances as pinch and designated hitters, they combined to bat .292 with 35 homers and 131 rbi in '83 alone.

It was also the year that the Birds collaborated with the Toronto Blue Jays at Memorial Stadium in what was, arguably, the most incredible and the most bizarre couple of innings in the entire history of Orioles baseball.

It all started late one Wednesday night (Aug 24) with two out and two on in the bottom of the 9th and the Orioles trailing, 3-1. From that point on, it was like magic, Orioles magic.

Suddenly a couple of back-to-back singles by Benny Ayala and Al Bumbry tied the score, and it was extra innings. With all the maneuvering he'd had to do in that inning, Altobelli was short of defensive replacements for the top of the 10th, so he had to improvise—big time. He put Lowenstein at 2nd base (for the first time in eight years), Gary Roenicke at 3rd base (for the first time in the majors) and little Lenn Sakata behind the plate (for

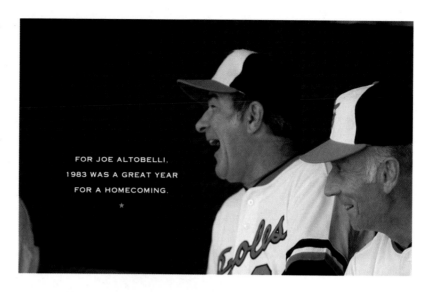

FOR JOE ALTOBELLI,
1983 WAS A GREAT YEAR
FOR A HOMECOMING.

★

the first time since Little League).

Big Bad Cliff Johnson, a long-time Orioles tormentor, led off the 10th for Toronto and planted one of Tim Stoddard's fast balls into the left field stands, advantage Blue Jays.

When the next hitter, Barry Bonnell, followed with a single, Stoddard left, and on came Tippy Martinez. As it turned out, Tippy never retired a batter. He didn't have to. First he picked off Bonnell. Then he walked Jesse Barfield, and picked him off. The next batter was Willie Upshaw and he singled. What happened next? Yep, you guessed it, Tippy picked him off also, and the Birds were out of the inning, though no one was quite sure how. Somebody quipped afterward, that the reason Tippy threw over to 1st so often in that inning was because Eddie Murray was one of the few guys around the infield he recognized.

Well, at least it had been entertaining, but that didn't obscure the fact that the Orioles again trailed by one. Not for long, however. Cal Junior led off with a game-tying home run, and by now every-

(LEFT) TIPPY, JOE ALTOBELLI AND INSTANT
CATCHER LENN SAKATA DEVISING THEIR
PICKOFF STRATEGY.

★

(RIGHT) LITTLE LENNY ACKNOWLEDGES THE
FANS TRIBUTE. HIS GAME-WINNING HOMER
SENT THEM HOME HAPPY, THOUGH EMOTION-
ALLY EXHAUSTED.

★

EARL GETS THE
FINGER.

★

body in the park was emotionally exhausted. Then along came Lenn Sakata to send them home to bed, on a 3-run game-winning homer off Joey McLaughlin. It had been a big day for Little Lenn, and the Orioles.

AN ORIOLES FAN
ON OPENING DAY
WITH A MOST
PROPHETIC SIGN.

★

To make it even more dramatic, the loss was the first in extra innings for the Blue Jays in exactly one year. They'd won 12 overtime games in a row.

The next night, the game was scoreless thru 9, then Barry Bonnell hit a 10th-inning homer to give the Jays a 1-0 lead. It was a bad omen for Toronto. In the bottom of the 10th, with one out and two aboard, "Disco" Dan Ford rammed a double into right center scoring Joe Nolan and Al Bumbry with the tying and winning runs. It was that kind of year for the O's.

There was (and is) something special about the relationship between the Orioles and their fans. The great Phillies third baseman, Mike Schmidt,

noticed it during the World Series in 1983. He said, "I've been booed all year here in Philadelphia. In Baltimore, Eddie Murray can go 0-for-24, and the next time up the fans will chant, 'Ed-die, Ed-die.'"

Scott McGregor, author of the shutout that clinched the world championship for the Orioles at Veterans Stadium, had been aware of that special feeling for a long time. After the game which earned the Orioles their third World Series Trophy, he was asked if that victory was his biggest reward in baseball.

"No," he said thoughtfully, "Playing for the Orioles in Baltimore these last seven years has been my biggest reward. This is just icing on the cake."

SCOTT MCGREGOR...
PLAYING HERE WAS HIS
BIGGEST REWARD.

★

THE Lost Weekend

A Glorious Near Miss

BY JIM HENNEMAN

One of the most memorable weekends in Memorial Stadium history developed from a most improbable setting.

The year was 1982. Earl Weaver had announced his retirement before the start of the season, prompting Howard Cosell to warn of the perils of a lame-duck manager.

That phrase would become a rallying cry at the finish, but seemed to have substance as the Orioles typically tip-toed their way through the first half of the season. With two weeks to go, there was little hope that Weaver would go out in style. A late run in September, also typical, appeared destined to come up short, and there appeared little hope that the Orioles could overtake the front-running Milwaukee Brewers. Even Weaver, the perennial optimist, seemed resigned to his fate of an inglorious ending to what had been a spectacular career.

As the impending end of his career became more of a story than the pennant-race itself, Weaver was asked to reflect more on the past than the immediate future. With less than a week remaining in the season, without knowing the complexities that would be involved, he agreed to an unusual request — to allow this writer to be with him throughout the day to document his final hours as manager of the Orioles.

It was a commitment Weaver kept, despite the ensuing circumstances that made that day, Oct. 3, one of the most incredible in Orioles' history. But we're getting ahead of the story.

As late as Aug. 22, the Orioles trailed the Brewers by 7 1/2 games. A 10-game winning streak helped narrow the gap and on Sept. 16, after a five-game sweep of the Yankees, the Orioles trailed by only one. With seven of the last 10 games scheduled to be played against the Brewers, the frenzy began to build — only to be dashed by four losses to the Tigers in a span of seven days.

"All we want is a shot at Milwaukee," said relief pitcher Tippy Martinez, the victim of a ninth-inning homerun by John Wockenfuss that left the Orioles on the brink after a 3-2 loss in Detroit Sept. 29. "I think it would be a great series and the fans would really enjoy it — if we can just get out of Detroit alive."

THE BIRD, BEARING BROOM, URGES THE O'S ON TOWARD A "CLEAN SWEEP".

★

With five games remaining, the Orioles were four games behind and on the verge of elimination when they rallied for four runs in the ninth inning to beat Detroit the next day. Meanwhile, Milwaukee lost in Boston to set up the tumultuous four-game series on the final weekend of the season.

Three games out with four to play. The Orioles needed a sweep to win, while the Brewers needed only one victory to survive. But the Orioles had gotten their wish — to return home with a chance, however slim, to overtake the Brewers.

"I wanted to win that game (against the Tigers) for all the people who had bought tickets for Friday night's double-header," Weaver said after the Orioles escaped from Detroit with their division title hopes intact. "Now I want to win the doubleheader for all the people who bought tickets for Saturday's game. And Saturday I want to win for all the people who bought tickets for Sunday's game.

"And Sunday," said Weaver, "I want to win for all of us." Ten days before, anticipating a final showdown, Milwaukee manager Harvey Kuenn had juggled his rotation so the recently acquired Don Sutton would be available to pitch the final game. The Brewers' pitching staff was struggling, with relief ace Rollie Fingers on the shelf, but "Harvey's Wallbangers," as Kuenn's sluggers were known, definitely held the upper hand.

"I don't know what the odds would be on that (an Orioles' sweep), but I know which way I'd bet," said Milwaukee centerfielder Gorman Thomas.

"It will be nice to do it (clinch the division title) head to head," said Paul Molitor, the instigator of the Brewers' potent offense.

There were 51,883 screaming fans, the second largest crowd in Memorial Stadium history at the

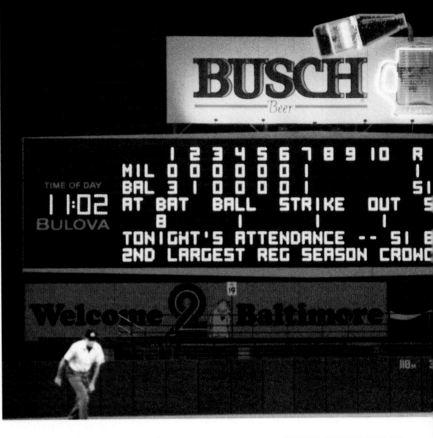

time, on hand for the Oct. 1 double-header. They watched righthanders Dennis Martinez and Storm Davis control the games as the Orioles systematically demolished the Brewers by the scores of 8-3 and 7-1.

It was a particularly poignant moment in the career of Martinez, who beat the Brewers for the second time in five days. Only two weeks before he had been in his native Nicaragua for the funeral of his father, who had died tragically after being hit by a bus. The next day it was more of the same for the Orioles and 47,235 spectators. With reliever Sammy Stewart shutting the Brewers down over the last 5 2/3 innings, the Orioles enjoyed another cakewalk, an 11-3 triumph that reduced the season to one game, winner take all.

It would be only the fourth time in history that two teams met on the final day of the regular season, with a championship hanging in the balance.

To get to that point the Orioles had to win 34 of 44 games leading up to the finale. Eddie Murray (.316, 32 home runs, 110 runs batted in) was as close as he would ever get to an American League MVP award. The first baseman's performance inspired a memorable line from veteran pinch-hitter Terry Crowley. "Eddie Murray owns this league," Crowley said in admiration. "He just lets the rest of us play in it."

Cal Ripken (.264, 28, 93) was en route to

THE O'S ON THEIR WAY TO A 7-1 WIN AND A SWEEP OF THE FRIDAY NIGHT DOUBLEHEADER BEFORE THE 2ND LARGEST REGULAR SEASON CROWD EVER (AT THAT TIME). THE BIRDS WERE NOW JUST ONE GAME BACK OF THE DIVISION LEADING BREWERS.

★

★

GENERAL MANAGER HANK PETERS' ORIOLES FINISHED 1ST OR 2ND 5 STRAIGHT YEARS FROM '79 THROUGH '83.

Rookie of the Year honors. John Lowenstein and Gary Roenicke would combine for a staggering 45 home runs and 140 RBIs. Unheralded Jim Dwyer had reached base safely 13 straight times, three short of Ted Williams' all-time record, going into the final game of the season.

Yet this was a season that produced a statistic even more remarkable than those personal accomplishments. It would be the only time in Weaver's career, the first time since 1967, that the Orioles

would play a complete schedule without a 20-game winner. But they went into that final game with their all-time winner, a pitcher who eight times had won 20 games in a season and was headed for the Hall Of Fame. The 1982 season turned out to be the last hurrah for Jim Palmer, but his personal 10-game win streak en route to a 15-5 record had helped the Orioles stay on course in the final six weeks.

"I think it's a dream, coming down to one game — a shoot-out with Jim Palmer against Don Sutton." Weaver had said from the outset that he'd be satisfied to get to the last day, with Palmer pitching for all the marbles — but he wasn't the manager who uttered that quote after the next-to-last game of the season. Instead it was Kuenn who uttered that assessment, after a hastily arranged team meeting that many interpreted as a sign of panic by the Brewers.

As the final day dawned, Weaver couldn't help but notice the irony of the situation. Here he was prepared for his final regular season game, and the man who hired him as a big league manager, Harry Dalton, was now the general manager of the team he had to beat to win a division title.

The Orioles had captivated the city of Baltimore with their stirring late season drive and Memorial Stadium was already alive when Weaver arrived four hours before game time on Oct. 3. Three weeks before he had been honored in emotional pre-game ceremonies

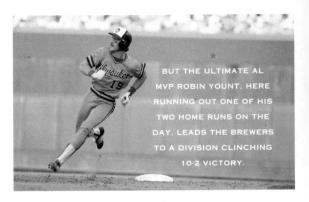

on "Thanks, Earl" day, and he was hoping there was at least one more win left to go into the record book. "There's one person who knows how it's all going to turn out," Weaver said in the midst of the pre-game chaos. "All we're going to do is act it out, so the rest of the world will know."

When Cosell walked onto the field in preparation for ABC's national telecast, he was mercilessly taunted from the stands because of his earlier references to Weaver as a lame-duck manager. "Win one for the duck," had become a rallying cry ever since the line was first used by second baseman Rich Dauer after a stirring clubhouse speech by the late owner Edward Bennett Williams in Boston on Aug. 14.

"Get out of there Howard, you don't have to put up with that," muttered Weaver, who enjoyed a good relationship with Cosell and would later become his broadcast partner.

Weaver fidgeted as the minutes dragged by, and finally returned to his office for an hour of solitude before the first pitch would be thrown. There was a knock on the door and Weaver looked up to see a friendly, but unfamiliar face. "Earl as an 87-year old native, I just had to come by and wish you luck," he said. "Baltimore has gotten so much publicity because of this day — I just wanted to come in and thank you."

With that, the man shook Weaver's hand, turned and left. Nobody knew who he was, or how he had

managed his way into the clubhouse. "I guess age does have its privileges," Weaver said with a smile.

Then, there wasn't anything left but the game. And shortly after it started, there wasn't much left but the memories.

On this day, Palmer didn't have one more great start left in that marvelous arm. He gave up only four hits in five innings, but three of them were home runs. Two of them were hit by Robin Yount (who would steal the thunder — and Murray's MVP award) in his first two at-bats.

Five runs in the ninth made it official. The Brewers would win, 10-2, but in the stands an amazing thing was happening. People refused to leave. They cheered wildly, though the dream was over. They applauded a team and its leader to such a point that the game became secondary.

"Forget what is happening on the field," said Cosell in his post-game commentary. "The real story is taking place in the stands."

On this weekend, the fans indeed ultimately became the story. They demanded a curtain call, then another. A full half-hour after the game had ended, after Weaver had concluded his final press conference, there were still 25,000 people in the stands. One last time, Weaver went back on the field — and led the crowd in a final O-R-I-O-L-E-S cheer. It took him another two hours to leave the park and head to a pre-arranged dinner with some friends.

When the night ended, it did so under a brilliantly full moon — perhaps the sure sign that the cycle was complete. Weaver would later return to manage the Orioles for part of 1985 and the entire 1986 season, but it wasn't the same. In a lot of ways, nothing has been the same since that final, frantic, frenzied weekend of the 1982 season. Some things you just can't recapture.

*The game was over,
yet the magic continued
(as described by Howard Cosell).*

"You are bearing witness to one of the most remarkable scenes, maybe that you'll ever see in sports. Yes, the fans have stayed. They have stayed to cheer. The defeat will hurt. There's Harvey Kuenn over to congratulate him, and Earl Weaver is crying. You can understand it. Very rarely has there been a scene like this, if ever. These people of this city, a city that has become a beautiful city under a brilliant mayor with an inner harbor equivalent with Boston. And there is Edward Bennett Williams, the owner, the great criminal attorney. And there they are standing and chanting, all of them in unison. And the sign says it all. Good-bye, Earl. And you deserve it. You've been one of the greatest managers in the history of the game."

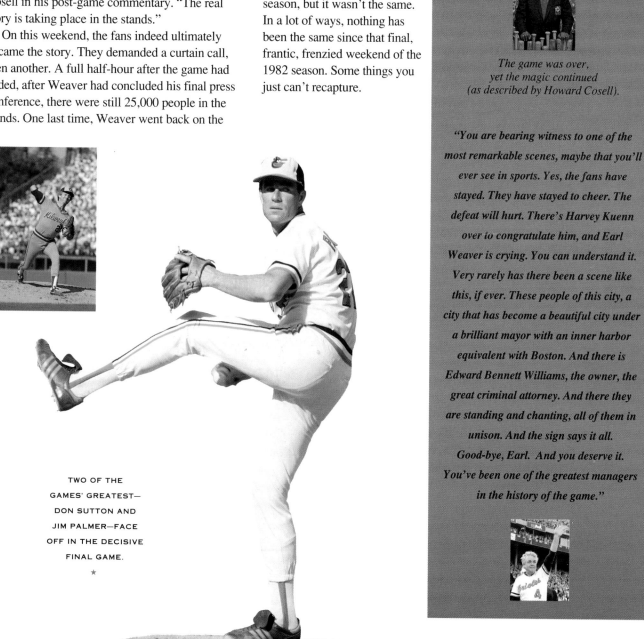

TWO OF THE
GAMES' GREATEST—
DON SUTTON AND
JIM PALMER—FACE
OFF IN THE DECISIVE
FINAL GAME.

★

Memorial Stadium INSCRIPTIONS

*The inscription on the front of Memorial Stadium,
as illustrated on the cover, and the five plaques,
mounted on the walls in its main lobby, say much about
our city and about many of the heroes of our time.*

Presidential Visits

I took 26 years and the Washington Senators move to Texas to get a sitting president to come to an Orioles game at Memorial Stadium.

Richard M. Nixon threw out the first ball on two historic occasions—Opening Day '54 and the '58 All-Star Game—but he was only the vice-president at the time. During his administration, his wife, children and son-in-law (David Eisenhower) came often, but never the man himself.

★

AFTER THROWING OUT THE FIRST BALL FOR THE '84 OPENER, PRESIDENT REAGAN GIVES ORIOLES CATCHER RICK DEMPSEY AN ENCOURAGING PAT. THE TWO HAD TALKED ON THE PHONE THE PREVIOUS OCTOBER AFTER THE ORIOLES BEAT THE PHILLIES IN THE WORLD SERIES.

Finally, in 1979, President Jimmy Carter came to the seventh game of the World Series, sat in the front row of boxes on the 3rd base side, and stayed to the end, graciously visiting the winning and losing clubhouses after the game.

President Ronald Reagan attended the opening game of the '83 World Series and two opening days, '84 and '86, while extending the Orioles streak to 4 straight losses before incumbent

★

PRESIDENT BUSH POPPED INTO THE ORIOLES CLUBHOUSE IN AN AUGUST '89 VISIT TO MEET SOME OF THE ORIOLES (FROM LEFT): JEFF BALLARD, DAVE SCHMIDT, PETE HARNISCH, STEVE FINLEY, JAY TIBBS AND DAVE JOHNSON.

chief executives at home.

On opening day '84, Mr. Reagan, after the first ball ceremonies, chose to sit in the Orioles dugout to watch the game, accompanied by Orioles owner Edward Bennett Williams and Commissioner Bowie Kuhn. During the first inning, the White House Press photographers, who know a unique photo opportunity when they see one, positioned themselves on the warning track in front of the dugout, snapping countless shots of the President and Messrs Williams and Kuhn.

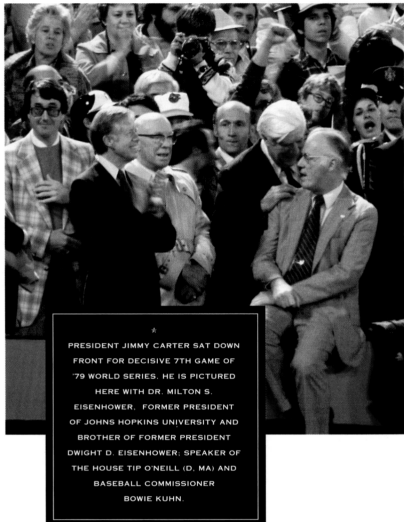

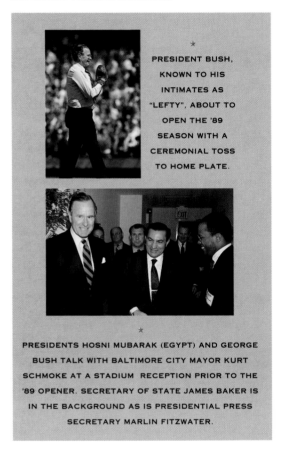

PRESIDENT BUSH, KNOWN TO HIS INTIMATES AS "LEFTY", ABOUT TO OPEN THE '89 SEASON WITH A CEREMONIAL TOSS TO HOME PLATE.

PRESIDENTS HOSNI MUBARAK (EGYPT) AND GEORGE BUSH TALK WITH BALTIMORE CITY MAYOR KURT SCHMOKE AT A STADIUM RECEPTION PRIOR TO THE '89 OPENER. SECRETARY OF STATE JAMES BAKER IS IN THE BACKGROUND AS IS PRESIDENTIAL PRESS SECRETARY MARLIN FITZWATER.

PRESIDENT JIMMY CARTER SAT DOWN FRONT FOR DECISIVE 7TH GAME OF '79 WORLD SERIES. HE IS PICTURED HERE WITH DR. MILTON S. EISENHOWER, FORMER PRESIDENT OF JOHNS HOPKINS UNIVERSITY AND BROTHER OF FORMER PRESIDENT DWIGHT D. EISENHOWER; SPEAKER OF THE HOUSE TIP O'NEILL (D, MA) AND BASEBALL COMMISSIONER BOWIE KUHN.

OPENING DAY '84- PRESIDENT REAGAN SHARES A STORY WITH COMMISSIONER BOWIE KUHN, ORIOLES HALL OF FAMER AL BUMBRY AND CLUB OWNER EDWARD BENNETT WILLIAMS.

Joe Altobelli, the manager of the defending world champions, couldn't see the field for the cameramen, but he didn't miss much, not of a positive nature at least. After the first inning, the President departed and things returned to normal, but by this time the O's were already down by 3-0 enroute to a 5-2 loss to the White Sox.

President Bush, unlike his two immediate predecessors, has seen the Orioles at their best...They went 3-1 during his first four official visits here ('89-'90), and in 1989 set what is believed to be a major league record. When he brought Egyptian President Hosni Mubarak to the '89 opener, it marked the first time in the Baseball's glorious history that two national chief executives (each from a different continent) had attended the same ball game.

IN Transition

BY GORDON BEARD

The impending crash of the Orioles during the mid-'80s was almost imperceptible at the outset.

But, following a crushing defeat in an Aug 6, 1986 game which featured two grand slams by the surging Orioles in one inning, the once insidious downturn became an avalanche.

Suddenly, the old Orioles' magic was gone, and so was the once Midas touch of Earl Weaver, who had been lured out of retirement in an effort to jump start a team already in transition.

Weaver, who ended 2 1/2 years of retirement to replace Joe Altobelli as manager on June 14, 1985, appeared to have rediscovered the winning formula in 1986 when the O's moved to within 2 1/2 games of first-place Boston on Aug 5 and seemed poised for one of their patented stretch drives.

The resurgence continued the next night when grand slams by Larry Sheets and Jim Dwyer in the fourth inning rallied the O's to an 11-6 lead after trailing 6-0. But, Toby Harrah later hit a slam for Texas, the Rangers won 13-11, and the O's went into a tailspin that lasted more than two seasons.

After going 18-9 during their previous 27 games, the Orioles went 14-42 the rest of the season, and finished last for the first time in

★

GRAND SLAM SLUGGERS: LARRY SHEETS, THE RANGERS' TOBY HARRAH AND JIM DWYER ALL HIT BASES LOADED HOMERS ON AUG. 6 1986 IN A GAME THAT PRECIPITATED THE ORIOLES' 14-42 END OF SEASON DEMISE.

IN A NOVEMBER '87 PRESS CONFERENCE, CLUB OWNER EDWARD BENNETT WILLIAMS INITIATED A RE-STRUCTURING PROCESS IN THE FRONT OFFICE. SHOWN HERE (L TO R): DIRECTOR OF MINOR LEAGUE PLAYER PERSONNEL DOUG MELVIN; NEW GENERAL MANAGER ROLAND HEMOND, WILLIAMS, SPECIAL ASSISTANT TO THE PRESIDENT FRANK ROBINSON; MANAGER CAL RIPKEN AND VICE PRESIDENT CALVIN HILL.

history...just three years after playing in their sixth World Series in 18 seasons. That ended a string of 18 straight winning seasons, second only to the 39 in a row posted by the New York Yankees, 1926-64.

About a month later, Weaver announced he would not return for 1987. He was succeeded by Cal Ripken Sr. who wound up 6th (67-95). Cal was replaced by Frank Robinson after the first six games of 1988, a season which began with the O's losing their first 21 games, and ended with the O's in last place again (54-107).

Through it all, however, the Orioles never lacked for fan support. Even though they were 102-139 at home during their three worst seasons, their attendance averaged 1,823,203.

Incredibly, a crowd of 50,402 was on hand to greet them at Memorial Stadium on Fantastic Fans Night when they returned home on May 2, 1988 with a 1-23 record.

An indomitable fan in the top corner of left field's upper deck displayed a white banner which read: "139-23."

The O's had no chance of winning all their remaining games to reach the record that the sign suggested, but they did defeat Texas 9-4 to cap one

★

FRED LYNN WON 3 GAMES WITH "SUDDEN DEATH" HOMERS IN '85.

of the most memorable days in club history.

Earlier in the day, a tearful Scott McGregor, long one of the team's best pitchers, said farewell after being released...one of the last moves in the dismantling of the 1983 world championship team. And, while saying goodbye to a star of the past, the Orioles looked toward the future.

Just before the game, Maryland Gov. William Donald Schaefer took the field and electrified the crowd by announcing that club owner Edward Bennett Willliams and the Maryland Stadium Authority had agreed on a 15-year lease for a new downtown ballpark that was expected to be ready for the 1992 season. A five-year option would carry thru the year 2011.

Williams acknowleged the cheers of the crowd from his skybox while attending the last Orioles' game he would ever see in person. The world renowned Washington attorney, who bought the club on Nov 1, 1979, passed away on Aug 13, following a long and courageous fight against cancer. The Orioles' family also had been shocked a little more than a month earlier when they lost their beloved trainer Ralph Salvon due to complications following heart surgery.

The idea for Fantastic Fans Night was contrived by WBAL-AM Radio and the Orioles' promotion staff. An added boost came from radio disc jockey Bob Rivers, who vowed to broadcast non-stop until the Orioles won. He stayed on the air at 98 Rock for 238 1/2 hours until the end of what was to become the longest season-opening losing streak in history.

Attendance for the season reached 1,660,738, the most for a team that lost 100 or more games.

The fans, apparently, were confident that the reorganization and redirection of the club, initiated by owner Williams just nine months before his death, would be a course that eventually would reverse the team's performance on the field.

The slide of the Orioles began innocently enough, even though their record of 85-77 in 1984 marked the first time they failed to win 90 games since 1976 (except for the strike shortened 1981 season).

The Orioles were still the best of the four returning division champions, and a record 35-5 start by the Detroit Tigers which left the O's 13 1/2 games behind by May 24, helped hide any obvious

★

THE RIPKEN PHENOMENON

★

THE ORIOLES MEDIA
GUIDE COVER FOR 1985,
FEATURING A FAREWELL
TRIBUTE TO JIM PALMER,
AL BUMBRY AND KEN
SINGLETON.

THE INVISIBLE ORIOLES MAGIC BAND: RICK
DEMPSEY SINGING LEAD; MIKE BODDICKER ON
GUITAR; EDDIE MURRAY ON DRUMS; RICH BORDI
ON ELECTRIC BASS, AND TRAINER RALPH
SALVON HANDLING BOTH THE KEY BOARD AND
THE SAX, BANGS OUT "THAT OLD TIME ROCK &
ROLL." DESPITE TOUGH TIMES THE ORIOLES
DIDN'T LOSE THEIR SENSE OF HUMOR.

★

signs of slippage.

The O's dipped only slightly to 83-78 in 1985, but the transition of the team was already well underway. In a 14-month period thru December, 1985, 13 players, the manager and two coaches from the 1983 world championship club had departed.

Hall of Fame pitcher Jim Palmer led the exodus, retiring at a tearful news conference on May 17, 1984. Mainstays Al Bumbry and Ken Singleton were not resigned after that season, and John Lowenstein and Dan Ford left early in 1985. After that season, Rich Dauer was not resigned, and trades disposed of Gary Roenicke and Sammy Stewart.

The 1985 season had started on a promising note, with the Orioles in first place for 19 of the first 35 days. They won eight games in "sudden death" at home that season, three on homers by Fred Lynn.

Lynn sank the Minnesota Twins on consecutive days, May 10-11, hitting ninth inning homers off Ron Davis and Curt Wardle, and the O's were first with an 18-9 record.

From that point on, however, the O's went 65-69. The return of Weaver caused a momentary stir, with a walkup ticket sale of 14,000 for his first game back, but not much changed on the field.

After their 1986 surge hit a brick wall, the Orioles finished at 73-89. In 1987, the year of the rabbit ball, they dipped further to 67-95 while becoming the first club ever to hit (211) and allow (a major league record 226) more than 200 homers in a single season.

If nothing else, Memorial Stadium fans were taking home a lot of souvenirs. In the three seasons ending in 1987, a major league high of 614 home runs had been hit in the old ballyard.

Edward Bennett Williams had seen enough. A month after the 1987 season ended, he made 12 significant personnel changes, including the hiring of Roland Hemond to replace Hank Peters as general manager. He also put the Orioles on a rebuilding program that would concentrate on player development within the system.

"This is not the beginning of the end," Williams said, drawing on a quote from Winston Churchill, "but the end of the beginning."

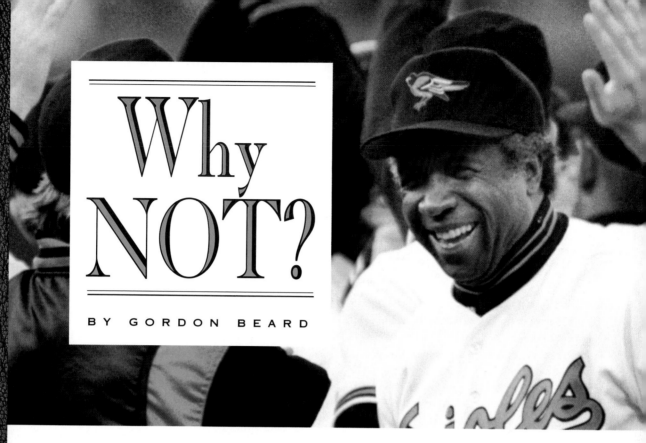

Why NOT?

BY GORDON BEARD

The Orioles weren't expected to perform any miracles when they embarked on the long comeback trail to respectability in 1989, but the courageous band of overachievers came within an eyelash of immortality.

With an 87-75 record that represented an incredible 32 1/2-game turnaround, the O's came within two victories of becoming the first major league team in the 20th Century to win a championship after finishing last the previous season.

At best, the Orioles were expected to win a few more games than in 1988 and finish a "higher last." But, as the season unfolded, they confounded the "experts" who had made them a concensus pick to finish last in the AL East.

The Orioles had a hard time convincing their skeptics, who expected they would begin to fade at any moment, but fans couldn't control their mounting enthusiasm.

About the time the O's had opened a 7 1/2-game lead by July 18, cryptic "Why Not?" signs began to appear in Memorial Stadium, and the club smartly picked up on the theme by having local musicians record a "Why Not?" rock tune. That added to the nightly frenzy on 33rd Street.

Crowds turned out in increasingly high numbers, and by season's end the home attendance reached a record high 2,535,208. Along the way, the underdog O's had even become America's team, as well, gaining widespread

support with their improbable feats.

After all, the club had posted progressively fewer wins in the previous five consecutive seasons, a major league record, reaching rock bottom with a 54-107 mark in 1988.

While finishing last for the second time in three years, a whopping 109 games below .500 since Aug 6, 1986, the '88 O's were last in the major leagues in batting (.232), runs (550) and earned run average (4.54).

What's more, they began the 1989 season with their youngest roster (average age, 27 years, 2 months) since 1968, including six rookies and six other players with less than two years of major league experience.

No wonder, then, that 170 of the 186 writers polled by The Sporting News for their pre-season predictions had picked the Orioles to finish seventh and last. Only five thought they could finish as high as fifth.

"We're not expecting miracles," club president Larry Lucchino conceded at the start of what was to be a tedious rebuilding era. "We just want to see improvement, not so much in the won-lost record, but in terms of a return to fundamentals."

"In my mind," General Manager Roland Hemond reflected after the season, "I had hoped that we would pass one club."

If the O's heard their bosses,

shortstop ever to hit that many in eight straight seasons.

Another bizarre outfield incident, this one working against the O's, came in the ninth inning of a June 14 night game when New York's Ken Phelps lifted a routine fly to left. Phil Bradley of the O's lost the ball in a dense fog, it fell safely, and two runs scored to give the Yanks a 2-1 win.

A month later, on July 15, the skies were clear but the ball was just as difficult to follow. That night, Mike Devereaux hit a drive down the leftfield line that even slow-motion replays failed to clarify.

Umpire Jim Joyce called it fair, and the O's won 11-9. California Manager Doug Rader went berserk, and was ejected some 14 hours later by Ken Kaiser when he rehashed his objections to the call while presenting lineup cards the next afternoon. The O's won that game, 3-2, on another close call, Mickey Tettleton's 11th inning drive on the rightfield line.

The Orioles didn't go unscathed in umpire confrontations. Frank Robinson, the American League's Manager of the Year, was ejected on Sep 13 in a dispute over the playing condition of the field following a 49-minute rain delay in the fourth inning, with the O's trailing 2-0. Before departing the scene, however, Frank faced the umpires, doffed his cap, and artfully executed several bows.

they weren't paying attention. As it turned out, they spent 116 days in first place before being eliminated on the next-to-last day of the season following a pair of one-run losses to the champion Toronto Blue Jays.

Before the miracle run ended, the O's had used 113 different lineups and 13 rookies, who accounted for a win and/or a save in 50 victories and produced 266 runs on offense. Memorial Stadium was rocking, not only to the "Why Not?" tune, but to the beat of a 47-34 home record that emphatically ended three straight losing seasons (102-139) in Baltimore. And, some of the things happening on the field were as bizarre as the club's turnaround.

Anyone who was in the park on Sep 4, and paying attention, will ever forget the play by Cleveland centerfielder Brad Komminsk, who leaped high in the air to backhand a drive by Cal Ripken Jr.

Komminsk appeared to have thwarted Cal's home run bid, but as he jackknifed over the fence ("back... back... HE'S out of here"), Komminsk couldn't hold the ball.

An admiring Joe Carter, the Cleveland leftfielder, called the effort by Komminsk, "the greatest catch NEVER made," and Cal wound up with his 20th homer, becoming the first

BOB MILACKI

JOE ORSULAK

BEN MCDONALD

JEFF BALLARD

GREGG OLSON

Richie Garcia, who had tossed Frank, later gave him high marks for the goodbye performance.

By contrast, rookie Dave Johnson said "hello" to his hometown fans, pitching a complete game, 6-1 victory over Minnesota in his Memorial Stadium debut on Aug 8 with hundreds of friends and family members in the stands.

Another rookie, Bob Milacki, beat the Twins 3-0 on April 23, and pitched the Orioles into first place for the first time since May 11, 1985. Milacki threw only 100 pitches and faced the minimum 27 batters, joining Jim Palmer ('67) and Mike Flanagan ('82) as the only Orioles to accomplish that feat.

At the other end of the spectrum, 12 pitchers delivered 501 pitches in a game that went 5:23 and ended at 1 a.m. on Sunday, Aug 13. Boston won 10-8 on Rich Gedman's 13th inning double.

The O's made more judicious use of their time on June 15, turning their first triple play in 10 years, only their fifth ever at home. Cal Ripken snared Steve Balboni's first inning liner, tossed to brother Bill at second to double Steve Sax, and the relay to Randy Milligan at first retired Don Mattingly.

While O's reliever Gregg Olson was on the way to winning the Rookie of the Year award, yet another first-round draft pick of the O's had an auspicious major league debut. Ben McDonald's very first pitch, in relief on Sep 6, resulted in a double play grounder off the bat of Cleveland's Cory Snyder.

It was, indeed, a year of surprises, but Manager Robinson kept things in perspective.

"This year was lightning in a bottle." he said. "The next step is don't get complacent and don't get fooled by the success of the ballclub. We still have a lot of work to do. Being in the race was much more of a bonus than I thought we might enjoy, but the organization has not lost sight of the fact that we're rebuilding. We've made a good start."

The accuracy of Frank's assessment was amplified in 1990, when the O's dropped to fifth place with a 76-85 record after a rash of late injuries exposed their lack of depth.

The Orioles entered August in third place, only four games out of first place. But, within a span of 15 days, they lost to the disabled list their leading hitter (Bill Ripken), their top home run hitter (Randy Milligan), their winningest pitcher (Dave Johnson) and their most active reliever (Mark Williamson). The August record of 9-18 was the second worst in club history.

The late slump cost the O's at the gate, still the home attendance of 2,415,189 was second only to the wonderfully wacky 1989 season. A turnout of 167,456 for a Boston series, June 15-18, set a club record for a four-game home series.

Those who did go thru the turnstiles, before and after the damaging injuries, were treated a 9-1 record in extra inning games and another set of lasting Memorial Stadium memories:

—Dave Johnson's 4-2 victory over Detroit in the delayed Apr 19 Opening Day, in the first Baltimore opener ever started by a hometowner.

—Phil Bradley's inside-the-park homer on June 8 against New York, the first in Baltimore since 1974, and the first by an Oriole in 14 years.

—Family Night on Sep 3, with Cal Sr., Cal Jr. and Bill in uniform for the Orioles, and the father-son duo of Ken Griffey Sr. and Ken Jr. playing for Seattle.

—The Orioles had four runners thrown out at the plate in a series against California, Sep 7-9, but swept the three games.

All in all, considering the injuries, it was another satisfying rebuilding year for the Orioles. The future looked bright as the Memorial Stadium era began to draw to a close and the club, as well as Orioles fans everywhere, looked forward to more successes and more memories at the new downtown ball-park, starting in 1992.

MIKE DEVEREAUX

THE Last Opening Day

BY BOB BROWN

It was the 38th and final...and warmest...opening day at Memorial Stadium. By game time, over-dressed opening day regulars, accustomed to a little more bite in the April wind-chill factor, were already complaining about the heat. The temperature in the press box was a torrid 89 degrees.

There was a sense of history in the air, and the crowd arrived earlier than normal, despite traffic problems. Orioles game programs, bearing "The Last Opening Day...April 8, 1991," on the front cover apparently appealed to both collectors and

historians. They were gone before game time, and a novelty stand on the main concourse behind home plate advertising "Memorial Stadium Memories" was under continuous attack all day long.

Outside, on the Venable parking lot across 33rd Street from the ballpark, the Brothers Berry, Kevin and Doug, a couple of Montgomery County builders involved in the new downtown ballpark project, arrived, and erected a 16 foot square plywood deck over their two vans. Before the stadium gates had even opened they had

**THE BERRY BROTHERS ENTERTAIN FRIENDS
WITHOUT TICKETS ON STADIUM PARKING LOT.**

★

hooked up their barbecue grill and 19 inch tv set (powered by a portable generator) and were entertaining friends who had been unable to get tickets.

Elsewhere on the stadium lots, the traditional Dixieland band serenaded one and all, and the ubiquitous television crews interviewed everyone in sight. In an annual rite of spring, plainclothes police arrested the usual ticket scalper suspects, and hauled them off to Northern District Headquarters.

Along with the weather, there were two other principal highlights on this last opening day: the pre-game show and the bottom of the first inning.

During the ceremonies "Ironman" Ernie Tyler, the Orioles' "field attendant" ("ballman") for the past 31 years and father of 11 including Orioles clubhouse managers Jimmy and Freddy, took a well deserved bow for never having missed a game since he first accepted the assignment on opening day 1960.

Another longtime Oriole, retiring Head Groundskeeper Pat Santarone, said goodbye while handing his rake to successor Paul Zwaska.

The Vice President of the United States, Dan Quayle, threw out one first ball. And, so did a couple of gracious veterans who had done this before, some 37 seasons earlier, when they started for their respective teams in the first game ever played here—Virgil Trucks for the White Sox and Bob Turley for the Orioles. They had flown to Baltimore for the occasion the night before from their homes in Florida, on Turley's plane.

Patriotism and the recent Persian Gulf War were principal themes of this opening day celebration. There were color guards from each of the five services; an additional unit from Ft. Meade, Maryland bearing flags from the 50 states and six territories; and five veterans from the recent war in the Middle East, here as personal guests of the vice president.

Army Staff Sergeant Delores King Williams, a Maryland native, sang the

(LEFT) VICE PRESIDENT DAN QUAYLE DELIVERS FIRST PITCH TO BOB MELVIN.

★

national anthem, and Secretary of Defense Dick Cheney, a major contributor to the success of Operation Desert Storm, drew what most agreed was the second biggest ovation of the afternoon.

However, it was the warm, emotional welcome accorded the return of an old friend that evoked what will undoubtedly be the most permanent memory of that day. When his name was called during the player introductions, the affectionate response was loud, and long.

Mike Flanagan, a transplanted New Englander, hadn't really left, despite the trade that sent him to the Toronto Blue Jays four seasons previous. He had continued to make his home in Baltimore, but somehow being back in an Orioles uniform seemed to confirm his continuing presence.

He had won 139 games and a Cy Young Award on his earlier tour with the Orioles, but it was the man more than the pitcher that endeared him to this community, and they let him know it. The Mike Flanagan Family won't soon forget Opening Day 1991.

There were some other interesting reactions during the pre-

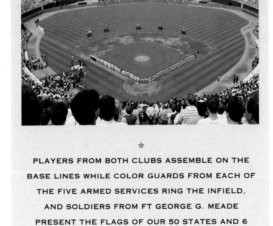

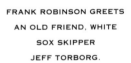

game ceremonies:

Jon Miller's introduction of White Sox captain Ozzie Guillen, triggered a rippling of boos throughout this unusually savvy opening day crowd, from fans who remembered bitterly that Guillen, not Cal Ripken, had won the American League's Gold Glove at shortstop the year before.

Several White Sox players standing on the first base line, spontaneously applauded the introduction of two Orioles in particular, Frank Robinson and Cal Junior.

Glenn Davis who came from Houston

where opening day is not such a big deal received a warm welcome, and a home town favorite, Ellie Hendricks, celebrating his 23rd opening day in an Orioles uniform, accepted enthusiastic plaudits while warming up Jeff Ballard in the bullpen.

For the record, the four umpires that afternoon— Jeff Evans, Shawn Kimball, Scott McDougall and Pete DeFlesco—all with minor league umpiring experience, were officiating their first, and probably last major league game. They were substitutes for the regular major league arbiters whose labor difficulties with

OPENING DAY 1954 STARTERS BOB TURLEY AND VIRGIL TRUCKS ALSO CHIP IN WITH CEREMONIAL FIRST BALLS.

★

EIGHT ORIGINALS, CELEBRATING THEIR 38TH YEAR WITH THE ORIOLES: SEATED: JOHN SANSONE, JOE CODD, JOE HAMPER, CHARLIE JASPER... STANDING: BORGIA COHEN, GERRY SIEGEL, FORMER INTERNATIONAL LEAGUE ORIOLE ERNIE SALAMONE AND HILARY "REDS" BERTLING.

MIKE FLANAGAN ACKNOWLEDGES AN ENTHUSIASTIC WELCOME HOME RECEPTION.

★

★

SECRETARY OF DEFENSE DICK CHENEY DRAWS A ROUSING OVATION. MARILYN QUAYLE, WIFE OF THE VICE PRESIDENT, JOINS IN.

baseball had not been settled until late the night before. The new kids did just fine.

The bottom of the first inning produced the first Orioles run of the year, and as it turned out the last of the day, on a Cal Ripken single and a double by newcomer Glenn Davis in his first official plate appearance as an Oriole. To that point it had been a nearly perfect afternoon.

But #29 the villainous righthander in visiting club gray, Jack McDowell, dueling for the first time with former Stanford University teammate, #29 Jeff Ballard, would yield only two more hits the rest of the way. And a White Sox outfielder named

Sammy Sosa, from the baseball capital of the world (San Pedro de Macoris in the Dominican Republic), hit two home runs that accounted for five rbi, far more than enough to assure an opening day loss for the home team. The final score was 9-1.

But, Opening Day 1991, as forgettable as the game might have been for Orioles fans, produced its share of lasting memories for the 50,213 on hand just as did each of the 37 that preceded it at Memorial Stadium dating back to 1954. It will be the same next year and beyond in the new downtown ballpark. There is something very special about Opening Day, particularly here in Baltimore.

JACK MCDOWELL ALLOWS
ONLY 2 HITS AFTER THE
1ST INNING.

★

★

NEWCOMER GLENN DAVIS (LEFT)
SINGLES FIRST TIME UP SCORING
CAL RIPKEN WITH THE ORIOLES 1ST
RUN OF THE YEAR AND LAST
OF THE DAY.

O pening Day, it turned out, was a harbinger of things to come. While the crowds continued large and lively throughout the season, the Orioles as a club could never quite produce a sustained winning effort.

On the field, it was a year of frustration, often contradicted by the brilliance of Cal Ripken Junior, whose virtuoso performance from start to finish was the best in the major leagues.

There was one statistic that perhaps revealed the plight of first Frank Robinson, then John Oates, more clearly than any other: In 42 games, the Orioles found themselves trailing by 3-0 or worse before the fourth inning. The club's record in those games? 4-38.

So Long, Farewell, Goodbye

BY BOB BROWN

And, then there were only three Memorial Days left. It was time for the final weekend, and on 33rd Street a kind of fever spread among those who clicked through the stadium turnstiles. Fueled by nostalgia, it brought tears to grownup eyes at the slightest recollection of a golden moment in the rich Memorial Stadium past.

On Friday before the game, some former International League Orioles were introduced, and so were a handful of the Orioles play-by-play broadcasters over the years. The biggest fireworks display in stadium history followed the final out.

On Saturday, fans entering the ballpark were shocked, but pleased to see current Orioles players, coaches, Manager John Oates, and several front office brass handing out free 15-month Orioles calendars.

The pre-game featured the introduction of the Baltimore Sun-Orioles All-Time Lineup, and between innings more than 200 ballpark items were given away; like the bases, Frank Robinson's "here" flag, the players' clubhouse chairs and the pitching rubber. It was also that historic day on which the Orioles would win for the last time at Memorial Stadium, a victory for Jim Poole and a save for Williamson. The big blow was a bases-loaded triple by Brady Anderson.

Finally the sun rose on the last day, nippy but pleasant and, best of all, no rain.

It was Sunday, October 6th, and no one who was there that day will ever forget it. The beloved Ellie Hendricks was honored for having spent more time in an Orioles uniform than anyone in club history.

times than good, but baseball lovers from all over this region called Birdland kept pouring into the ballpark. In early August, the Orioles had averaged only one win in every three home games, but everytime they opened the gates an average of 32,000 faithful flooded in. The worse the Orioles played, it seemed, the more determined were their fans to show their support, seemingly unfazed by the frustration of 47 losses in games decided by one or two runs.

In early September, the pace of the season that had seemed so interminable in the early and middle going, accelerated as the countdown of "Memorial Days" began to approach zero.

In mid-month, the Orioles and their fans paid a moving tribute to their former brothers in arms, the Baltimore Colts, a celebration that brought out the still active Colt Band, and a host of former players including Football Hall of Famers John Unitas, Jim Parker, Lenny Moore and Art Donovan.